To Barbara Hufsmith

Vladimir Vukanovic

Vladimir Vukanovic

SCIENCE AND FAITH

SCIENCE AND FAITH

Vladimir Vukanovic is a physical chemist, with a Ph.D. in physics. He was Professor of Physical Chemistry, University of Belgrade, Yugoslavia, later Visiting Professor at Columbia University, New York, NY and at RIT -- Rochester Institute of Technology, Rochester, NY. He is now Distinguished Professor Emeritus RIT. He has done scientific research in atomic spectroscopy and plasma chemistry and is the author of many scientific publications.

Light and Life Publishing
P.O. Box 26421
Minneapolis, Minnesota 55426-0421

Copyright © 1995
Vladimir Vukanovic
Library of Congress Card No. 94-73519

All right reserved. No part of this book may be reproduced, stored in a retrieval system, or transmitted in any form or by any means, electronic, mechanical, photocopying, recording, or otherwise, without the written permission of Light and Life Publishing Company.

ISBN 1-880971-06-2

CONTENTS

PREFACE 1

INTRODUCTION 3

ORDER 9
   General Remarks 9
   Scientists On Order In Nature and On God 11
   Awareness of Order in Nature 32

EVOLVING UNIVERSE 39
   The Universe, Its History and Its Future 39
   Two Opposite General Directions 48
   The Anthropic Principle 52
   Levels of Cosmic Evolution 57
   "From Being to Becoming" and "Order Out of Chaos" ... 61
   Holism, Novelty, Reductionism 66
   Necessity and Chance; the Idea of Opposites 68
   Life 72
   God and Evolution of the Universe 76
   Human Beings as God's Collaborators 81
   Time 83

CONCLUSION 89
   Science Motivates My Belief in God 89
   Love 93

REFERENCES 97

SELECT BIBLIOGRAPHY 103

INDEX OF AUTHORS 111

PREFACE

If you were ever taught that science undermines belief in God, you are the one I had especially in mind when writing this book; for it is just the opposite: science motivates belief.

You may be interested in the quotations about science and religion from many well-known scientists. To be a scientist, to think deeply about phenomena in nature, often means to be religious.

You may also be interested in two basic facts which we learn from science :

First, nature demonstrates rationality, an orderly arrangement.

Second, there is constant change in nature, and one direction of this change leads to evolution, from the simple to the more complex.

I have included a little information about the scientists quoted and theories mentioned, which might be known to you or just of no interest. The material in small print will make it easier for you to skip over it. As you might expect, there is less information about scientists born in this century.

In 1990, 1991 and 1992 I gave lectures to the students of St. Vladimir's Orthodox Theological Seminary, Crestwood, New York, about religion and science; the material of these lectures is partly incorporated in the book.

My education in physical chemistry and physics, but not in biology and other sciences, has influenced my approach to the subject of this book.

Vladimir Vukanovic

Powers of ten

You probably know that: 10^2 means 100 (1 and 2 zero); 10^3 means 1000 (1 and 3 zero); $10^4 = 10000$ etc. and that 10^{-2} means $1/100$; 10^{-3} means $1/1000$; $10^{-4} = 1/10000$ etc.

SCIENCE AND FAITH

INTRODUCTION

We should like to understand the world in which we live. Where do nature's processes lead? Are natural phenomena connected? What can we tell about the enormous universe in which we live? What is its purpose? What is the purpose of our life and what is our destiny? There is a deep, very strong desire in all of us to find answers to these questions.

Many things give us a partial answer: there is the beauty of nature and art; philosophy; service to humanity and our capacity to feel love. Love has an absolute positive value in any culture, any society, any economic conditions. Many attempts to find the answers center upon religion and science.

Is there a discrepancy between scientific and religious truth? Or do they support each other? Could these two pictures of the world, religious and scientific, inhabit completely different compartments within us, without influencing each other?

Religion and science follow different paths in our longing for the truth, but still they have much in common.

Science conducts observations, makes measurements, experiments, calculations. Science recognizes an orderly pattern in nature and formulates physical laws which combine many phenomena in mathematical equations. Science is based on acceptance of the fact that an orderly pattern objectively exists in nature. There is a rationality in the world which we can to some extent comprehend. Science brings an awareness of a fundamental order in the world, an order which makes it possible for the world to exist and evolve.

To understand that the world's phenomena do not exist haphazardly, but follow some principles, some laws, has a deep meaning. Those principles which we discover in nature appeal to us as ideas of how the world is arranged. To someone with little scientific knowledge the world may look chaotic; to the scientists it

SCIENCE AND FAITH

will appear more orderly. Many well-known physicists have religious convictions because of their scientific knowledge.

The existence of this orderly arrangement leads to an approach to religion through science. Another approach is related to the cosmic evolution. Matter constantly changes; to recognize the direction of these changes is very important from the religious point of view. These two approaches will be explored in this book.

Questions of ethics, of compassion, of charity are related to religion. However, ethics is very important in scientific research. It is hardly possible for a scientist to achieve success without personal integrity and total honesty. Technology without an ethical base can be a terrible evil.

Religion starts with faith in God, the creator and sustainer of the world Who is also love;

God is love (First Letter of John 4/8, 16) [1]

The definition that God is love also means that He is the origin of moral imperatives.

Religion also considers that knowledge of God may be received by understanding the world in which we live, from the observation of nature.

"Ever since God created the world, His invisible qualities, both His eternal power and His divine nature, have been clearly seen : they are perceived in the things that God has made." (Letter of Paul to the Romans 1/20) [1]

Also :

**"The heavens are telling the glory of God;
and the firmament proclaims his handiwork.
Day to day pours forth speech,
and night to night declares knowledge.
There is no speech, nor are there words;
their voice is not heard;
yet their voice goes out through all the earth,
and their words to the end of the world."
(Psalms 19/1-4) [2]**

Chapter 1 — Introduction

Nature speaks to us; we must "listen" and attempt to understand. From the many who have spoken about two kinds of God's revelation, I quote **Mikhail Lomonosov** (1711-1765):

> "The Creator gave the human race two books. In one He revealed His majesty, in the other - His will. The first is the visible world which He created so that man - beholding the magnitude, the beauty, and the harmony of His creation - could acknowledge God's omnipotence. The second book is Holy Scripture." [3]

Lomonosov was a scientist, poet and grammarian. He worked in physics, astronomy, geology. He contributed to the founding of Moscow University.

The importance of an approach to religion through reason was expressed by **Blaise Pascal:**

> "Those to whom God has imparted religion by intuition are very fortunate and justly convinced. But to those who do not have it, we can give it only by reasoning, waiting for God to give them spiritual insight....." [4]

Blaise Pascal (1623-1662), physicist and mathematician, philosopher, writer on religious subjects, published his first scientific paper when he was only 16 years old. His work on the laws of probability, on pressure in liquid and air, among other things, gave him a good scientific reputation in his youth. He spent the last years of his life in a monastery writing theological treatises.

Our religious and scientific pictures of the world influence each other. A model of "separate compartments" may work only to some extent, for we cannot split our personalities. **John Polkinghorne,** a theoretical physicist and ordained priest, President of Queens' College, Cambridge, England, and author of several books on science and religion, said in one of his recent lectures:

> "I stand before you as somebody who is both a physicist and a priest, and I want to hold together my scientific and my religious insights and experiences. I want to hold them together, as far as I am able, without dishonesty and without compartmentalism. I don't want to be a priest on Sunday and a physicist on Monday; I want to be both on both days." [5]

SCIENCE AND FAITH

Discussing science and religion, it is important not to think of God as the "God-of-the-gaps", that is, not to expect Him only in the unknown and the inexplicable. We label phenomena in nature which we can ascribe to physical laws "scientifically explicable" and do not look for God's activity there. We tend to say : there are many things which science cannot explain to-day; perhaps science will explain them tomorrow, perhaps never. Well, we tend to say : God acts here. True enough, God's action is everywhere, including in those phenomena upon which science can shed light, in natural laws and constants, in the evolution of the universe, including the evolution of life on Earth.

Richard Bube, professor of Material Science and Electrical Engineering at Stanford University, California, wrote in several articles against the attempt to speak of the "God-of-the-gaps, " and many writers have agreed with him.

Prof. Richard Bube is known in the USA for his work in the American Scientific Affiliation which publishes the journal : "Perspective on Science and Christian Faith".

Bube based his thoughts about this on the writings of **Dietrich Bonhoeffer** ("Letters and papers from prison"), a priest who died in a concentration camp during the Second World War:

"I should like to speak of God not on the boundaries but in the center, not in weakness but in strength, and therefore not in death and guilt but in man's life and goodness." [6]

A remark may be made about the search for a concordance between the scientific and religious pictures of the world. Science develops. Scientists of different epochs have different understandings of nature. Scientific theories of this century differ from those of the last one. Scientific thoughts in the twenty-first century will undoubtedly differ from those of to-day. Can we then talk about a concordance between scientific and religious understanding of the world?

Probably, yes, only we should not become lost among details of scientific interpretations of natural phenomena, but simply look for the common denominator in scientific ideas. *For such common denominators we can take just those two understandings of nature which*

Chapter 1 — Introduction

lead our thoughts to religion. As mentioned, we should like to base an approach to religion on two scientific statements: *the existence of an orderly pattern in nature, and the direction of the evolution of the universe.* Science of any century is unthinkable without the understanding that an orderly pattern exists in nature. There may be some differences in describing the order, but its existence cannot be denied. It is true that the idea of an evolving universe has only been fully developed and accepted in this century. Again, there are some disagreements among theories of the history of the universe and predictions for its future, but the evolution of the universe looks like an indisputable fact. It is reasonable to take it as a common denominator as well.

Behind the orderly pattern in nature, behind the direction of the cosmic evolution, many scientists see God. Their understanding of nature may be partial, insufficient, unclear, but the feeling that God is closer because of their research, brings a wonderful excitement and has a deep religious meaning. This excitement can be shared by anybody with a limited scientific knowledge.

Imagine that a number of scientists are in a building with many multi-colored windows. Depending upon where they are, which methods they use and which angles of observation they have, they see either blue, yellow or red light. However, they all know that the color they see is related to the bright light outside and the awareness of this creates a deep thrill.

The English poet Percy Bysshe Shelley (Adonais, LII) wrote :

"The One remains, the many change and pass;
Heaven's light forever shines, Earth's shadows fly,
Life, like a dome of many-coloured glass
Stains the white radiance of Eternity." [7]

What a joy, what a deep religious experience it is to have a presentiment about "the white radiance of Eternity."

SCIENCE AND FAITH

ORDER

General Remarks

Science is not only the accumulation of facts about nature, neither is it an artificial systematization of the observed facts. Many phenomena are intrinsically related to the common pattern, to some rational order in nature. *Science is based on the understanding and acceptance of the existence of a rationality in nature and its consistency.* Scientists try to express this common pattern through natural laws, and a great variety of phenomena can be related to a small number of laws.

It is true that our understanding of rationality in the world depends upon our angle of observation - like that of the scientists described on the previous page. It is true that their comprehension of natural laws depends on the general knowledge available at any given moment in scientific development. It is also true that there is some subjectivity in our conclusions about phenomena in the world around us. As we shall later discuss, quantum mechanics indicates that the scientist who does the experiment is a part of the experiment and hence the result depends upon him/her as well.

Nevertheless, despite the incompleteness of our knowledge, despite possible imperfections in the formulation of natural laws and their limited validity, despite the inevitable subjectivity, the existence of an objective rationality in nature is without doubt. There is no reason to suppose that orderly patterns, discovered laws, the world's rationality - have just been invented by humans. The theoretical physicist **Walter Heitler** wrote :

"The law permeates matter. Human beings understand the law, but did not create it." [8]

Prof. Walter Heitler taught 1941-1949 at the Dublin Institute for Advanced Studies, and after 1949 at the University of Zürich, Switzerland. As a quantum physicist he worked also on the explanation of chemical bonding; this work

SCIENCE AND FAITH

especially brought him international recognition. Several books on science and religion enhanced his reputation. His profound, logical thoughts, expressed simply, strongly pull his readers towards an approach to religion through science.

The existence of orderly patterns in nature is for many an indication that the world is not made at random but according to a plan, according to divine foresight. How moving it is for anyone who, through scientific knowledge, comes closer to understanding this plan. What a special joy it is for a scientist who, through his or her discoveries, may feel in touch with ideas of how the world is arranged, and begin to see God through His creation. I shall illustrate this by many quotations. First let us hear the physicist **Friedrich Dessauer**:

"The discovery of natural law is a meeting with God." [9]

Prof. Friedrich Dessauer (1881-1963) is especially known for his work in biophysics. He wrote several books in which he expressed his deeply religious feelings, his humanism and thoughts about the relation between science and religion.

Albert Einstein (1879-1955) expressed his understanding of the orderly arrangement of the world like this:

"This firm belief, a belief bound up with deep feeling, in a superior mind that reveals itself in the world of experience, represents my conception of God." [10]

"A knowledge of something we cannot penetrate, our perceptions of the profoundest reason and the most radiant beauty, which only in their most primitive forms are accessible to our minds - it is this knowledge and this emotion that constitute true religiosity; in this sense and in this sense alone, I am a deeply religious man." [11]

And speaking of the scientist with a profound scientific mind, he said:

"His religious feeling takes the form of a rapturous amazement at the harmony of natural law, which reveals an intelligence of such superiority that, compared with it, all the systematic thinking and acting of human beings is an utterly insignificant reflection." [12]

Chapter 2 — Order

We may say: science discovers orderly patterns in nature and expresses them through natural laws which we relate to God's idea of how the world is arranged. Or we may say : a fundamental orderly arrangement exists in nature, as an expression of God's wisdom; we grasp some aspects of this arrangement in the described natural laws. The idea about a fundamental order in nature may embrace not only natural laws but also, as we shall later see, the initial conditions of the universe, values of natural constants, the holistic understanding of the universe, the interplay of necessity and chance in the evolving universe. Fundamental order could include all modes of God's creation in this meaningful universe, all modes of God's guidance of the cosmic evolution, all God's activity in the universe. Still, God is greater than that.

Let us first concentrate on the words of scientists, most of them eminent physicists, explaining how their understanding of order in nature motivated their religious feelings. There is a similarity in their thinking and their strong convictions. The philosopher **Baruch Spinoza** expresses the opinion of many scientists:

> **"The more we know of things, the more we know of God."** [13]

Scientists On Order In Nature and On God

Here are some thoughts about God expressed by scientists of different epochs. Many of these thoughts express the excitement they felt at seeing through their work the order in nature and God as its creator.

Nikolaj Kopernik /Nikolai Copernicus/ (1473-1543):

> **"Through steady observation and a meaningful contact with the divine order of the world's structure, arranged by God's wisdom, – who would not be guided to admire the Builder who creates all!"** [14]

Johannes Kepler (1571-1630) :

> **"Work on astronomy means reading God's thoughts."** [15]

> **"The (physical) laws are within the limits of the human spirit's capacity to comprehend; God's wish was to let us recognize them."** [16]

SCIENCE AND FAITH

"I thank thee, Lord God our Creator, that thou allowest me to see the beauty in thy work of creation." [17]

Kopernik gave us the heliocentric system which Kepler accepted. Kepler is known as a founder of dynamical astronomy. He said that planets move around the sun in elliptical paths, with the sun at one focus. Further, that a line between the sun and planets covers equal surfaces in equal times. Kepler was excited by the symmetry and simplicity in nature. He stressed the harmony in the solar system, particularly in his work "De Harmonice Mundi".

Both Kopernik and Kepler expressed their deep religious convictions strongly supported by their discoveries. Talking about Kepler, **Werner Heisenberg,** theoretical physicist, wrote:

"There can be no doubt that in this early phase of modern science the newly discovered conformity to mathematical law has become the true basis for its persuasive power. These mathematical laws, so we read in Kepler, are the visible expression of the divine will, and Kepler breaks into enthusiasm at the fact that he has been the first here to recognize the beauty of God's works. Thus the new way of thinking assuredly had nothing to do with any turn away from religion. If the new discoveries did in fact contradict the teachings of the Church at certain points, this could have little significance, seeing that it was possible to perceive with such immediacy the workings of God in nature." [18]

Walter Heitler, theoretical physicist, similarly said:

"A contradiction (between science and religion) is out of the question. What follows from science are, again and again, clear indications of God's activity which can be so strongly perceived that Kepler dared to say (for us it seems daring, not for him) that he 'could almost touch God with his hand in the Universe.'" [19]

Isaac Newton (1642-1727):

"The wonderful arrangement and harmony of the cosmos would only originate in the plan of an almighty and omniscient being. This is and remains my greatest comprehension." [20]

Chapter 2 — Order

Hardly anybody would deny that Isaac Newton belongs among the world's greatest physicists. Classical mechanics is based on his laws of motion. The first law, or the law of inertia, expresses the statement that a body continues in a state of rest or in uniform motion in a straight line unless it is constrained by a force to change its state. The second law is that the force is equal to a product between the mass of the body and its acceleration. The third law says that action is equal to reaction, the force acting by object A on an another object B is equal in magnitude and opposite in direction to the force acting by object B on the object A. Newton's second and third law of motion led to the law of the conservation of momentum (the product of the mass of a particle and its velocity). This law is one of the most fundamental in nature. The laws of motion are related to the law of gravity. Newton also gave us the basis of optical spectroscopy, demonstrating the spectrum of colors, which mixture gives white light.

Let us note the law of universal gravity (inverse square law):

$$f = G\frac{m_1 \times m_2}{r^2}$$

f - the force of gravitational attraction between body 1 and body 2, G - gravitational constant, m_1 and m_2 the masses of body 1 and body 2, r^2 - square of the distance between the centers of body 1 and body 2.

The law has an elegant simplicity and yet describes the movement of celestial bodies, of stars, planets, moons around planets, of satellites, of falling apples or stones on Earth.

Newton's excitement at coming through his work closer to "the plan of an almighty and omniscient being, " is typical for many scientists.

Newton's work has not lost its actuality to-day. A deeper insight into the question of gravity is given by Einstein in his theory of general relativity. But the simple equation for the gravitational attraction given by Newton is valid in a very good approximation also in the sun's system. Our work in science and technology is unthinkable without Newton's laws of mechanics.

However, understanding the connection between individual events differs to-day from Newton's physics which is deterministic. This deterministic view leads to the idea that if a genius knew all laws of physics, all conditions, everything happening in the world at a given moment, then this genius would also know the past and could predict the entire future. The development of science abounded in such strict determinism.

Gottfried Wielhelm Leibniz (1646-1716) :

"The order, the symmetry, the harmony enchant us...God is pure order. He is the originator of universal harmony." [21]

SCIENCE AND FAITH

Leibniz, philosopher and mathematician, also worked in physics, law and theology. He was one of the inventors of the differential and integral calculus, but mostly known as a philosopher.

Rudjer Boskovic (Ruggiero Boscovich) (1711-1787):

"The deepest intelligence of philosophy and science are inseparable from a religious view of the world." [22]

Boskovic was an astronomer, mathematician and physicist.

Karl von Linné (Carolus Linnaeus) (1707-1778):

"I saw passing by the eternal, endless, omniscient, almighty God, and in respect I knelt." [23]

Linné was a botanist who first defined the system for classifying and naming plants and animals.

William Herschel (1738-1822):

"The more science develops, the harder it is to reject the evidence of the eternal existence of creative and almighty wisdom." [24]

William Herschel was an astronomer known for his discovery of the planet Uranus.

André Marie Ampère (1775-1836):

"The most convincing evidence of God's existence is ...the evident harmony which maintains the order of the universe, and in which living beings find...what they need for their spiritual and physical development." [25]

Hans Oersted (1777-1851):

"Every thorough investigation of nature leads to perception of God...." [26]

Physicists Ampère and Oersted (the latter also a chemist)investigated the relation between electricity and magnetism and started a new part of physics - electromagnetism, which led to numerous technical applications.

The unit of electric current is called an ampere.

Karl Friedrich Gauss (1777-1855):

"When our last hour comes, we shall have unspeakably great joy, a joy of which we previously in our work had only a presentiment." [27]

It is often said that Gauss, Newton and Archimedes are the three greatest mathematicians of all time. There is an anecdote about Gauss. When he was

Chapter 2 — Order

12 years old, he distinguished himself so greatly in mathematics that his professor, Buttner by name, declared in class:"He is beyond me. I can teach him nothing more." He worked in various branches of mathematics including arithmetic and infinitesimal calculus. He also worked in astronomy and physics.

Jons Jacob Berzelius (1779-1848):

> "Everything linked with organic nature points to a wise purposefulness and appears to be the product of a superior intelligence..." [28]

Berzelius was a chemist known for his determination of atomic weights. He isolated several chemical elements.

Augustin Louis Cauchy (1789-1857):

> "I am a Christian which means that I believe in the deity of Christ, like Tycho de Brahe, Copernicus, Descartes, Newton, Leibnitz, Pascal ... like all the great astronomers and mathematicians of the past." [29]

A mathematician who worked also in astronomy and physics; he clarified the principles of calculus, originated the theory of permutation groups, contributed to the theory of functions of a complex variable.

Michael Faraday (1791-1867).

Faraday was a chemist and physicist. Phillip Eichman, a biologist, wrote about Faraday in a recently published article : "Michael Faraday:Man of God - Man of Science ":

> "Michael Faraday was a man of both tremendous religious faith and great scientific achievement. The central, guiding principle of his life was his faith in God as the creator." [30]

Among quotations about Faraday, which Eichman used in his article, let us choose one by J. F. Riley:

> "...the abounding humility with which he saw himself, not as a man raised by genius above his fellows but as one turning the pages of a book which is already written and finding therein order, pattern and design worthy of the Great Creator." [31]

Faraday discovered the laws of electrolysis. Many substances are dissociated in solutions, almost completely or partially, into particles which are electrically positive or negative: positive and negative ions. By putting electrodes in the solution and passing an electrical current through it,

SCIENCE AND FAITH

electrolysis occurs. Positive ions separate on the negative electrode and vice versa. Faraday's laws concern the weight of materials formed on electrodes. Faraday's laws, together with the experiments of Millikan and other researchers, led to the conclusion that a minimum amount of electrical charge existed in nature. This amount is regarded as one of the natural constants and corresponds to the electrical negative charge of an electron. Faraday's experiments also included liquefaction of chlorine, separation of benzene and development of stainless steel as well as work in electromagnetism. He made the first electric motor, dynamo and transformer.

Faraday's scientific ideas about electric and magnetic fields and lines of forces were, in a profound way, further developed by **James Clerk Maxwell** (1831-1879). Maxwell is especially known for his theory of electromagnetism. He developed sets of equations for the continuity of electric and magnetic fields and for their mutual interactions; both fields are linked together in an electromagnetic wave propagation. Maxwell described light as a type of electromagnetic waves. Faraday and Maxwell were friends and both were deeply religious men.

Lord Rayleigh (John William Strutt, 1842-1919) who succeeded Maxwell in the chair of experimental physics at Cambridge University, was also religious. He continued the study of electromagnetic waves, worked in optics and other areas of physics. He obtained the Nobel prize in 1904 as co-discoverer of gas argon.

Heinrich Maedler (1794-1874) :

"The serious researcher into nature cannot deny God."
"He who has looked deeply into God's workshop and has had an opportunity to admire the eternal wisdom, must bend his knee before the highest spirit." [32]

Maedler was the astronomer who first mapped the moon.

Charles Lyell (1797-1875):

"In whatever direction we go in our investigations, we discover everywhere the clearest proof of a creative intelligence, of its providence, wisdom and power." [33]

Lyell was a geologist. He suggested the division of the geological system into groups according to the ratio of recent to extinct species of shells : Eocene (dawn of recent), Miocene (less recent) and Pliocene (more recent). These names are generally accepted. He supported Charles Darwin's theory of the origin of species.

Justus von Liebig (1803-1873) :

"Only those who attempt to read from the mighty book

Chapter 2 — Order

which we call nature will actually recognize the greatness and infinite wisdom of the Creator. [34]

A chemist especially known for his work in organic and agricultural chemistry, Liebig observed that some chemical groups remained unchanged in different reactions, called them radicals and developed the theory of radicals. This theory contributed to the first attempt to systematize organic chemistry. Liebig also suggested the use of mineral fertilizers when some soil elements were depleted.

Robert Mayer (1814-1889):

"I end my life with the deep, heartfelt conviction that real, true natural science and philosophy must lead to faith in God and the Christian religion." [35]

Prescot James Joule (1818-1889):

"We meet a great variety of phenomena which speak in plain language of the wisdom and blessed hand of nature's great architect." [36]

William Kelvin, later Lord Thomson (1824-1907):

"Overwhelming evidences of an intelligence and benevolent intention surround us, show us the whole of nature through the work of a free will and teach us that all alive beings depend on an eternal creator-ruler." [37]

Walter Nernst (1864-1941), Nobel prize 1920 :

"To work in physics means to observe God's creation." [38]

Robert Mayer, James Joule, William Kelvin - Lord Thomson and Walter Nernst, together with several other physicists, are regarded as the founders of thermodynamics.

Robert Mayer, a physicist and physician, formulated the first law of thermodynamics. His work was not received sympathetically at first, and this depressed him greatly. However, he later received the title "von Mayer".

James Joule, a physicist, developed methods for measuring the interconvertibility of different forms of energy;he is known for determining "the mechanical equivalent of heat" related to the amount of work necessary to produce a unit of heat. He has given his name to the energy unit - a "joule". There was friendship and fruitful collaboration between him and Lord Thomson for many years.

SCIENCE AND FAITH

William Kelvin, Lord Thomson, a physicist, is known particularly for his work on the second law of thermodynamics. The so-called "absolute temperature scale", independent of the properties of any thermodynamic substance, is also called the Kelvin scale. The absolute zero of temperature, impossible to achieve, is - 273.15 °C. A Kelvin degree is equal to one Celsius degree, so the 0 point of the Celsius scale (32 °F) equals 273.15 Kelvin degrees.

Lord Thomson worked also in other areas of science such as telegraphy and geology. He achieved considerable fame in his lifetime, and was buried in Westminster Abbey.

Walter Nernst, a physical chemist, worked in electrochemistry, thermochemistry, the theory of solutions and photochemistry. He is regarded as one of the founders of modern physical chemistry. The first statement of the third law of thermodynamics was made by Nernst and is known as the "Nernst heat theorem": in any chemical reaction involving a pure, crystalline, solid substance, the change of entropy is zero at zero absolute temperature. Seven years later, Max Planck gave a slightly different formulation of this law.

Laws of Thermodynamics

The first law of thermodynamics says that the total amount of energy in an isolated system is constant, an isolated system being one in which there is no exchange of heat, work or matter with the surroundings. This is the law of energy conservation. Energy changes from one form to another, but its total quantity remains the same after all changes.

The second law of thermodynamics points to the degradation of energy, the decrease of the potential of a system to produce work. There are many postulations of the second law. One, according to Lord Thomson, says that it is impossible to have a cyclic process (in which the conditions are the same at the beginning and at the end) which will produce work taking heat only from one heat reservoir. There must be two reservoirs different in temperature. Heat can be taken from the reservoir at the higher temperature, but cannot be completely converted into work; a part will necessarily be used to increase the temperature of the reservoir with lower temperature. As a consequence, the temperature difference between the two reservoirs will be smaller.

Fundamentally, transfer of energy from higher to lower temperature is a spontaneous and irreversible process. The heat will be spontaneously transferred until equilibrium is achieved, when the temperature of both reservoirs will be the same. A description of this spontaneity gives a thermodynamic function called entropy. In a closed system entropy never decreases, but takes a maximum value in equilibrium. One way to understand entropy is through probability, relating it to the orderliness of the system. Increase in entropy means decrease in orderliness. We just saw an example : if we have two reservoirs with different temperatures and we connect them,

Chapter 2 — Order

the difference in temperature will vanish; the new system of two connected reservoirs will become less orderly when the two temperatures equalize. The process is irreversible.

All the time we see an increase of entropy around us. A broken glass will not spontaneously recombine. A house about which nobody cares will spontaneously become a ruin in time. Other forms of energy transform into heat, and heat dissipates into the surroundings. The differences in energy levels become smaller in time. Degeneration of energy advances in time; there is less potential for achievement.

The second law of thermodynamics is one of the most general natural laws. It applies to practically everything, to any kind of matter in any form; it does not even necessarily require a heat transfer.

However, the increase of entropy is not a fundamental law but has a statistical character. It can be applied only to a large number of particles. For individual molecules or atoms, even for a small number of them, the notion of entropy increase is meaningless.

Processes also occur in nature when more complex, more orderly forms arise without violating the second law of thermodynamics. The formation of orderly forms, a local decrease in entropy, is always accompanied by a total increase of entropy, taking into account the increase of entropy in the surroundings.

The third law of thermodynamics, as postulated by Max Planck, says that the entropy of a pure, crystalline substance is zero at zero absolute temperature on the Kelvin scale.

David Livingstone (1813-1873):

"Jesus is near you and sees you and He is so good and friendly." [39]

David Livingstone, explorer and geographer, was a very religious man. At the end of his life, very weak, he prayed daily. He was found dead kneeling at prayer in front of a burning candle.

Johannes Reinke (1849-1931):

"Nature appears to us not as a chaos of blind forces, not as a disorderly mix of energy and material particles; quite the opposite, order is plainly there.

To human beings lost on our planet, God's essence remains a deep mystery; however, the observation of nature leaves no doubt about the reality of His existence, which is transcendent and immanent at the same time." [40]

SCIENCE AND FAITH

Johannes Reinke was a botanist known particularly for his work on sea algae. He strongly believed in the harmony between science and religion.

Ernest Rutherford (1871-1937), Nobel prize 1908 :

"People who do not work in science are under the misapprehension that the scientist, because of his greater knowledge, must be irreligious; to the contrary, our work brings us nearer to God." [41]

Rutherford, a physicist, did research mostly in radioactivity and atomic structure. He used the results of scattering alpha radioactive particles on thin metal layers to develop an atomic model. (Alpha particles are the nuclei of helium atoms; some radioactive materials spontaneously emit alpha particles.)

Rutherford concluded that the size of a nucleus is about 10,000 times smaller than the atomic size, e.g. about 10^{-12} cm. (In the microworld, size does not have the same meaning as in the macroworld; the size of a nucleus means a domain where the existence of nuclear forces can be detected.) The nucleus has a positive electric charge which is compensated for by the total negative charge of the electrons surrounding it, so that the atoms as a whole are electrically neutral. The electric charge of a nucleus is equal to the product between the elementary electrical charge in nature and an integer. This integer represents the so-called "atomic number" which corresponds to the number of electrons in the atom.

Rutherford's atomic model is sometimes called the planetary model, because of its analogy with the sun system where planets rotate around the sun. This model enabled Niels Bohr to develop his atomic model which included the quantum processes in atoms.

Max von Laue (1879-1960), Nobel prize 1914:

"The best (physicists) have always deeply believed that scientific truth represents in one sense a 'glimpse' of God." [42]

Von Laue was a physicist who investigated the structure of crystals and the (electromagnetic) wave nature of X-ray radiation.

Robert Millikan (1868-1953), Nobel prize 1923:

"People who know little about science, and people who understand little about religion, could argue with each other, and observers might think this a dispute between science and religion, but actually, it would be a clash between two forms of ignorance." [43]

Millikan, a physicist, is best known for determining the value of the elementary electrical charge (a natural constant) which is the negative charge of an electron and positive one of a proton.

Chapter 2 — Order

Arthur Compton (1892-1962), Nobel prize 1927:

"Far from being in conflict with religion, science has become religion's ally. With increased understanding of nature we also learn about the God of nature and the role we play in the drama of the cosmos." [44]

Compton, a physicist, investigated the nature of electromagnetic radiation. The interpretation of his experiments, of the so-called Compton effect, shows the nature of electromagnetic radiation: radiation can be interpreted as an electromagnetic wave and/or as an assembly of particles of energy called photons;which properties come to expression depends on our experiment. (The scale of electromagnetic radiation includes : gama radioactive radiation, X-rays, UV radiation, visible light, infrared radiation, micro- and radio waves.)

Paul Sabatier (1854-1941), Nobel prize 1912 :

"Only people uneducated in either science or religion can think that they oppose each other." [45]

Sabatier was a chemist known for work on catalytic synthesis in organic chemistry.

Alexis Carrel (1873-1944), Nobel prize 1912 :

"A human being should also keep a struggling soul ... to search for light in the darkness of this world ... to aspire to grasp the invisible ground of the Universe." [46]

"A human being needs God as he needs water and air." [47]

Alexis Carrel was a physician known for his discoveries of antiseptic procedures in surgery and his cancer research.

Sir James Jeans (1877-1946) :

"Today there is a wide measure of agreement which, on the physical side of science, approaches almost to unanimity, that the stream of knowledge is leading towards a non-mechanical reality;the universe begins to look more like a great thought than like a great machine."

"We discover that the universe shows evidence of a designing or controlling power..." [48]

Sir James was a mathematician, physicist and astronomer. He worked on the kinetic theory of gases, on the distribution of energy in "black body"

SCIENCE AND FAITH

radiation and on many cosmological problems such as the formation of stars. (A "black body" emits maximum energy at any temperature and wave length.)

Heinrich Vogt (1890-1966) :

> "...There must be a mind which transcends matter, space, time and every level of existence, a mind which is infinitely higher than the human mind, a mind of divine nature, who created the world, who supports and guides it, now as He did in the dawn of creation's first day."[49]

Vogt was an astronomer who worked chiefly in astrophysics, cosmogony (theory of the creation of the universe) and cosmology (science of the universe). One theorem in astrophysics, relating to formation of stars, is named after him : Vogt-Russel.

Now come quotations from five scientists known for their work in quantum physics: Max Planck, Werner Heisenberg, Pascual Jordan, Walter Heitler and Erwin Schroedinger. Planck and Heitler have already been mentioned, but I should like you to know a little more about their views on science and religion.

Max Planck (1858-1947), Nobel prize 1918 :

> "We may conclude that from what science teaches us, there is in nature an order independent of man's existence, a meaningful order to which nature and man are subordinate.
>
> Both religion and science require faith in God.
>
> For believers, God is in the beginning, and for physicists He is at the end of all considerations. For the former, God is the basis, and for the latter, the crown of every observation of the world.
>
> When we ascribe to God the attributes of goodness and love in addition to almightiness and omniscience, then asylum in God offers to man, searching for consolation, a large measure of secure happiness.
>
> Wherever we look, we never find a contradiction between religion and science, rather complete accordance in all essential points.
>
> Both religion and science are parallel and reach the same destination in the remote future. To realize that, the best

Chapter 2 — Order

thing is to make a constant effort to understand the essence and the goal of science and religious faith. Then it will be more clear that, although methods differ, because science generally depends on reason and religion on belief, the sense and direction of progress completely agree.

Religion and science continually struggle together against skepticism and dogmatism, against atheism and superstition, and the motto which eternally indicates the direction of this struggle is: there, to God!" [50]

The revolutionary development of modern physics, as opposed to classical physics, started with Max Planck who was a religious man. At the beginning of this century he published the idea about the discontinuity in emission and absorption of energy; energy is emitted and absorbed in parts called quanta.

Werner Heisenberg (1901-1976), Nobel prize 1932 :

In "Positivism, Metaphysics and Religion", in his book "Physics and Beyond", Heisenberg related his conversation with Niels Bohr and Wolfgang Pauli (two eminent physicists) in Copenhagen. Here is an excerpt :

"Wolfgang asked me quite unexpectedly:

'Do you believe in a personal God?' ...

'May I rephrase your question?' I asked. 'I myself should prefer the following formulation: can you, or anyone else, reach the central order of things or events, whose existence seems beyond doubt, as directly as you can reach the soul of another human being? I am using the term 'soul' quite deliberately so as not to be misunderstood. If you put your question like that, I would say yes ...'

'In other words, you think that you can become aware of the central order with the same intensity as of the soul of another person?'

'Perhaps.'

'Why did you use the word 'soul' and not simply speak of another person?'

'Precisely because the word 'soul' refers to central order, to the inner core of a being whose outer manifestation may be highly diverse and pass our understanding.'"

SCIENCE AND FAITH

Earlier in their conversation, Heisenberg spoke about the "central order":

> "When people search for values, they are probably searching for the kind of actions that are in harmony with the central order.... In science, the central order can be recognized by the fact that we can use such metaphors as 'Nature has been made according to this plan.' It is in this context that my idea of truth impinges on the reality of religious experience."
>
> 'I can follow you most of the way, ' Wolfgang said, 'but just what do you mean when you say that the central order must win out ?....'
>
> 'By that I mean something altogether commonplace, for instance, the fact that as each winter passes, the flowers come into blossom in the meadows, and that as each war ends, cities are rebuilt. Time and again destruction makes way for order.'" [51]

Heisenberg and Einstein are, perhaps, the most prominent physicists of this century. Heisenberg is known for his work on matrix mechanics, one of the representations of quantum mechanics, and the formulation of the uncertainty principle. He also worked in atomic, molecular and nuclear physics. He gave the fundamental philosophical interpretation of quantum physics, together with Niels Bohr, the so-called Copenhagen interpretation.

Pascual Jordan (1902-1980):

> ..."materialistic natural philosophy is no longer in unison with the perception of natural science; in fact, it contradicts it." [52]

Pascual Jordan was a theoretical physicist especially known for his work in quantum physics. He made fundamental contributions to matrix mechanics with Heisenberg and Born and to quantum electrodynamics with Pauli, Klein and Wigner. He spoke to questions about gravity, to the general theory of relativity, cosmology and biophysics. In his opinion, modern physics removed any walls between a scientist and the spiritual sphere of religious belief.

Walter Heitler :

> "The world is infinite. We think neither about the physical-astronomical space of the universe, which is probably finite, or the duration of the physical universe.

Chapter 2 — Order

We think about the spiritual depth of the world, a depth which extends.... to God." [53]

Heitler a deeply religious man, considered that science motivates religion:

"From the first intuitive feeling of the Divine until the conviction of God's existence, science has an essential role." [53]

Erwin Schroedinger (1887-1961), Nobel prize 1933:

In his lectures, "Mind and Matter", given at Trinity College, Cambridge, in 1956, Schroedinger said:

"Physical theory in its present stage strongly suggests the indestructibility of Mind by Time." [54]

Schroedinger is known for his work in quantum physics, for the idea that the particles in microphysics have the qualities of both particles and waves. The "Schroedinger equation" is fundamental to wave mechanics, even fundamental to physics. He also worked on statistical thermodynamics and atomic spectra.

Some Words About the Quantum Theory

At the beginning of the twentieth century, Max Planck promulgated the revolutionary idea that the emission and absorption of energy occur in parts called quanta. (The idea about the corpuscular nature of light had already been aired by Newton.) Einstein's interpretation of the photo-electric effect (under given conditions, light can cause emission of electrons from some materials) strongly supported Planck's idea.

There are experiments which can be explained only if we ascribe a corpuscular nature to light. Other experiments can only be explained by its wave nature. It was similarly found that all particles in the microworld show a wave nature in some experiments. For example, the application of the wave nature of electrons is in the electron microscope. The "wave of matter" cannot be noticed in the macroworld because their wavelength reciprocally depends on the mass;if the mass is big, the wavelength is too short to be observed.

Niels Bohr had this to say about the complementary concepts of wave and particle :

> "It is often said that the quantum theory is unsatisfactory because, thanks to its complementary concept of 'wave' and 'particle', it prohibits all but a dualistic description of nature. Yet all those who have truly understood the quantum theory would never ever dream of calling it dualistic. They look upon it as a unified description of atomic phenomena, even though it has to wear different faces when it is applied to experiment and so has to be translated into everyday language. The

SCIENCE AND FAITH

quantum theory thus provides us with a striking illustration of the fact that we can fully understand a connection, though we can only speak of it in images and parables. In this case, the images and parables are by and large the classical concepts i.e. 'wave' and 'corpuscle'. They do not fully describe the real world and are, moreover, complementary in part, and hence contradictory. For all that, since we can only describe natural phenomena with our everyday language, we can only hope to grasp the real facts by means of these images." [55]

Niels Bohr introduced quantum reasoning into Rutherford's planetary atomic model. In Bohr's atomic model, electrons in atoms rotate at specific distances from the nucleus which correspond to quantum energy atomic levels.

In the farther development of quantum physics, the description of atomic systems can be found as a solution of the Schroedinger equation. The position of electrons is described in terms of probabilities. Electrons could be anywhere in atoms, but with a different probability. Objects in the microworld are generally described by wave mechanics in terms of probabilities; strict determinism is just not valid in the microworld.

The other representation of quantum mechanics is the matrix mechanics developed by Heisenberg, Jordan and others. Results about the properties of objects in the microworld obtained by wave mechanics and matrix mechanics are in complete agreement, although there are differences in starting points and mathematical procedures. Matrix mechanics abandons a pictorial model of atoms; mathematical analysis gives answers about atomic properties.

Heisenberg's uncertainty principle tell us about the uncertainties of some coupled values in a microsystem:

$$\Delta E \times \Delta t \geq h$$

$$\Delta p \times \Delta q \geq h$$

E – energy, ΔE – uncertainty of energy, t – time, Δt – uncertainty of time, $\geq$ – equal or bigger, p – impulse (= mv, impulse is the product of mass and velocity), Δp – uncertainty in impulse, q – co-ordinates of the position of the object, Δq – uncertainty in the position, h = Planck's constant, one of the fundamental natural constants.

This principle tells us that there is some uncertainty about the energy and time of a process. It also tells us that, if we know exactly the energy of the process, then the time at which it occurrs is quite uncertain; if we know exactly when a process occurs, it is impossible to tell anything about its energy. In a similar way the impulse and co-ordinates of the position of a quantum

Chapter 2 — Order

object are coupled. These uncertainties are not caused by the imperfection of the measuring system; they are intrinsic characteristics of the objects in the microworld.

The properties of an object in the microworld, observed by us, depend on the act of observation. The observed properties, i.e. the reality, is not an illusion;it exists, but what it is without the act of observation we cannot say. This has profound implications on the interpretation of quantum physics. Without going more deeply into this question, let me only stress the implications of subjectivity in our knowledge of the microworld.

Let me also mention the holistic approach in describing identical particles in an atomic system by the quantum theory. The helium atom consists of a nucleus and two electrons. Quantum mechanics does not distinguish two electrons, describing for example the behavior of electron 1 and electron 2, but gives solutions for the system as a whole.

More thoughts of **Albert Einstein** (1879-1955), Nobel prize 1921:

> **"He (the physicist) is astonished to notice how sublime order emerges from what appeared to be chaos. And this cannot be traced back to the working of his own mind but is due to a quality that is inherent in the world of perception." [56]**

When asked how he discovered his relativity theory, Einstein replied that he

> **"was so strongly convinced of the harmony of the universe." [57]**

> **"What is the meaning of human life or, for that matter, of the life of any creature? To know an answer to this question means to be religious. You ask: Does it make any sense then to pose this question? I answer: The man who regards his own life and that of his fellow creatures as meaningless is not merely unhappy but hardly fit for life." [58]**

Everyone has heard of Einstein. In 1905 he published four papers on 1) the special theory of relativity; 2) the equivalence of mass and energy; 3) the corpuscular nature of light (an interpretation of the photoelectric effect which strongly supported Max Planck's idea about the quanta of energy); 4) the Brownian motion (the motion of particles suspended in liquid, which can be explained by their interaction with molecules of liquid).

Some 10 years later he published the general theory of relativity which also represents the modern theory of gravity.

SCIENCE AND FAITH

After the fission of the uranium nucleus was discovered in 1939, it was understood that this process could be achieved in a chain reaction. During fission, as well as during the fusion of light nuclei, a part of the mass can be translated into energy, according to Einstein's equation :

$$E = mc^2$$

E - energy, m - mass which is transformed in energy, c - speed of light.

In a chain reaction, an enormous amount of energy can be liberated.

The statistical character of quantum physics did not correspond to Einstein's thoughts upon how the world is arranged;between the description of reality in terms of certainties or probabilities, he was for the former. Einstein also challenged Bohr's and Heisenberg's interpretation of quantum physics; he disagreed with the idea that the nature of things depends upon observation. He suggested experiments to prove his point, in vain as it turned out.

Einstein spent many years working on theories of the unification of the gravitational and electromagnetic fields as an expression of the geometrical properties of the entity : space-time. This work met with no success. However, the general trend to look for a deeper reality is appealing.

Einstein's God was not a personal one. He saw God in the coherence of the cosmos. He spoke of **a cosmic religion.**

Arthur Eddington (1882 - 1944) :

"Modern physics leads necessarily to God." [59]

Eddington, an astrophysicist, made important contributions to the theory of the solar system and the constitution of stars. He concluded that most stars are gaseous throughout. Eddington was an exponent of the theory of relativity and tried to unify the quantum theory and general theory of relativity. In 1919, he led an expedition to investigate the total solar eclipse, the results of which verified, for the first time, the predictions of the general theory of relativity.

Theory of Relativity

Special Theory of Relativity

The speed of light is constant - this is one of the natural constants. The speed of light is the same for all observers, independently of how fast they move.

We cannot talk about time without talking about space, nor space without time;they are one entity. We find it difficult to visualize any system for which it is necessary to have more than three coordinates (three for space and one for time);but we can work mathematically with such systems. There is no universal flow of time; no unique absolute time. Observers travelling at

Chapter 2 — Order

different speeds will measure time differently. An event which takes place at a specific point in time will be measured differently by the observers; and the assigned position of the event will be differently perceived. No one measurement is more correct than the other, but all measurements are related; any observer could calculate the measured time and position of the event determined by another observer if that observer's relative velocities were known.

A fast-moving clock will be slower than a slow-moving one, not because of some properties of the clock, but because of the nature of time itself. To illustrate this, let us consider experiments with muons, subatomic particles accelerated to a speed close to that of light. Muons have a mean period of life of about 10^{-6} second; after about 1 microsecond they disintegrate in the other particles. If accelerated to a very high-speed, however, their "life" is essentially prolonged.

We can imagine the "twins effect". One twin goes on a high speed journey through cosmos, the other waits on Earth. When the traveller returns home, he is some years younger than his twin brother.

While time is stretched for the high-speed traveller, space is shrunk.

The mass of an object increases if it moves at high speed. Nothing can travel at the speed of light. If it did, theory predicts, the object would have an infinite mass, which is impossible. The increase of the mass of atomic particles is again verified in accelerators.

For speeds common for us, the changes of time and space are negligible, but they are essential if velocities approach the speed of light.

One of the results of the special theory of relativity is the equivalence between energy and mass : $E = mc^2$.

The special theory of relativity does not take gravitational effects into account.

General Theory of Relativity

According to this theory, gravity is not a force like others but a consequence of distortion of space-time geometry. The subtle curvatures of the four dimensional space-time entity are related to gravity and due to the distribution of matter. "Space tells matter how to move;matter tells space how to curve"are a physicist's often quoted words. Space and time not only affect but also are affected by everything which happens in the universe. Everything in the universe depends on everything else; we must have a holistic concept of the universe for a part of it cannot be observed by itself.

Celestial bodies move in a curved space along a so-called geodesis, the shortest path between two points.

Newton's law of gravity, a simple inverse square law, can be regarded as an excellent approximation, valid in the case when the curvatures of the

SCIENCE AND FAITH

space-time entity are small, as in our solar system. Deviations from Newton's law occur when the bodies move in strong gravitational fields where the space-time entity is significantly curved.

However, the behavior of the planet Mercury has some anomaly if described by Newton's law, but it can be explained by the general theory of relativity.

There have been two theoretical predictions, both confirmed: the first was about the bending of light rays in gravitational fields, the second about the change of the frequency of light in gravitational fields.

The stronger gravity is, the more pronounced is the time warp. Time runs more slowly near massive bodies like Earth than in the cosmos where the gravitational field is small. Identical clocks, one on Earth and another at some distance from the Earth's surface, show different times.

On the surface of some stars with very strong gravity, we could expect time to slow down considerably. If the gravity were even stronger, such a star would collapse into a black hole.

Not everything is relative in the theory of relativity, neither the speed of light nor the charge of an electron nor other physical constants. Chemical reactions will presumably be the same for all observers. The principle of causality is not set aside: no effect can occur before the cause.

The theory of relativity contributed to the development of cosmology. We cannot talk about events in the universe without the notions of space and time;it is meaningless to talk about space and time beyond the limits of the universe. After the discovery of the universe's expansion, a theory of the uniform, expanding universe is established. The old idea of a universe which does not essentially change, which did and could exist for ever, is replaced by the concept of a dynamic, expanding, evolving universe. It seems that the universe began at some finite time in the past and may come to an end at a finite time in the future.

Michael (Mihailo) Pupin (1858 - 1935) :

"If cultured people had ... an intelligent view of the primary concepts in the fundamental sciences, there would be no need to renew periodically the tiresome topic of the alleged clash between science and religion". [60]

Pupin was a physicist and an inventor, notably of electrical devices, such as the long-distance telephone.

Guglielmo Marconi (1874 - 1937), Nobel prize 1909:

"Proudly I declare that I am a believer. I believe in the

Chapter 2 — Order

power of prayer. I believe it not only as a faithful Catholic but also as a scientist." [61]

A physicist, Marconi worked on radiotelegraphy and contributed to wireless communications over long distances.

Pierre Lecomte du Noüy (1883 - 1947):

"Those who tried to abolish the idea of God did a shameful and anti-scientific job.

I entered adult life with a scepticism fashionable at that time and it took thirty years of laboratory work to convince myself that I had been deliberately deceived by precisely those who had the obligation to enlighten me, if only by simply acknowledging their own ignorance.

I came to this belief following the paths of biology and physics; I am convinced that it is impossible for any thinking scientist not to come to this conclusion unless he is blind and dishonest." [62]

Lecompte du Noüy was a physician who worked in biophysics. During the First World War he worked on the physiology of healing wounds.

At the end of his life he said:

"I wrote my last book "L'homme et sa Destinée" deeply convinced that science without God will in our time destroy the world." [63]

Enrico Cantore :

"Fundamentally, the message of science is that nature makes sense. Indeed nature which, to a non-scientific person may appear largely chaotic, reveals itself to the scientist as inherently orderly.

The significance of nature, as revealed by science, amounts to the manifestation of an immensely powerful intelligence.... which, indeed, manifests itself in nature, but cannot be simply reduced to nature itself.... Science enables reflective man to perceive that the significance of nature somehow exceeds nature itself..." [64]

Cantore is a physicist, philosopher and theologian. His publications are related to humanism, science and religion. He is director of the World Institute of Scientific Humanism.

SCIENCE AND FAITH

Jack Lousma:

"We can see God on the small scale in the world around us. We can see Him on the large scale in the universe. But, most important, we can see Him in the effect He can have in our lives within us." [65]

Lousma, an astronaut and aeronautical engineer, was backup docking module pilot of the US flight crew for the historic Apollo-Soyuz mission in 1975, in which the first American-Soviet link-up took place in space.

Hubert Alyea:

"Science strengthens my religion. The more contact I have with the physical world, the more I believe in the reality of God." [66]

Aleya is professor of chemistry at Princeton University, USA.

Awareness of Order in Nature

As we have seen,

"for many scientists, exposure to the order of the universe, as well as to its beauty and complexity, is an occasion of wonder and reverence." – Ian Barbour, theologian, physicist and philosopher [67]

A scientist who comprehends the order in the world, who describes it in the most humble way but still "touches" the fundamental idea of how the world is arranged, has enormous satisfaction and excitement. His efforts and the time which he spends working, the money which he earns, are unimportant.

An awareness of the connection between particular phenomena and laws, natural principles, is not a privilege of scientists only; it can be shared by anyone with some scientific knowledge. *The understanding that many natural phenomena may be related to several fundamental laws is profound and remarkable.*

The order in nature is witnessed in natural laws. The validity of a natural law should be understood to be only approximate; their forms which we may discover tomorrow could embrace facts unknown to-day and contain even greater mathematical beauty. However, our understanding of the laws leads us to believe in nature's

Chapter 2 — Order

orderly arrangement created by an over-all superior Wisdom.

The fact that we can have some understanding of this order and rationality is itself remarkable. Again, to quote **Einstein:**

> **"The incomprehensible thing about the universe is that it is comprehensible."** [68]

God allows us some success in our effort to comprehend His design. That is the meaning of **Einstein's** following words:

> **"God is subtle, but He is not malicious."** [69]

John Gribbin, cosmologist and **Martin Rees,** leading theorist in astrophysics, Director of the Institute of Astronomy, Cambridge, UK, questioned the meaning of our ability to comprehend the order in nature :

> **"The astonishing triumph of modern science, especially physics and astronomy, is its ability to describe so many of the bewildering complexities of the natural world in terms of a few underlying principles."**

> **"Is it merely a coincidence that creatures intelligent enough to understand a few simple physical laws exist in a world where only those physical laws are needed to explain how everything works? Or is there some deeper plan that ensures that the universe is tailor-made for humankind?"** [70]

We accept the fact that natural laws and the order in nature which they express do not change in time. Yet the essential characteristic of matter is constant change. The law permeates matter and influences its change; but change in the physical state itself does not influence the law which is constant in character. No matter exists outside law; *yet the laws resemble ideas more than matter.*

The laws are the same throughout the universe. We think that those laws which we can often prove in our laboratories are valid everywhere else. This corresponds to our holistic view; if the universe is a whole, there cannot be different laws in its various parts. However, we cannot talk about the laws and natural constants in a black hole.

SCIENCE AND FAITH

Together with the initial conditions of the universe, natural laws and natural constants represent a base, a frame for the cosmic evolution. The same laws shape both the simple and the complex in the universe. The same laws permit the evolution of the universe from its plasma state to the formation of atomic nuclei, atoms, molecules, galaxies, stars and planets, and the evolution of life.

Natural laws are the expression of stability in the universe but not, as we shall discuss, cosmic tyranny. Providing a firm frame for cosmic evolution, they also allow some freedom. There is not a strict determinism in nature, there are rather novelties in the advancing cosmic evolution and a degree of unpredictability.

Can we, in principle, imagine a universe with different laws, or without such a coherence as in our universe, which led to life? Perhaps, theoretically, we could imagine such a universe, but what purpose would it have without life and love?

We have to distinguish two notions:
1) the connection between particular phenomena and a natural law upon which they are based and
2) reductionism.

The connection between the phenomena and the law indicates the orderly arrangement of the world. The word reductionism is used to express the possibility of explaining the properties of a level of the evolving cosmos with those of preceding levels.

For example, gravitational attraction is often used to express our awareness of the world's rationality. Many phenomena in the world are related to gravity. The attraction can be expressed by Newton's simple law; in a very good approximation, this law is valid in our sun system. The rotation of planets around the sun, the rotation of moons, the ocean tides, the motion of satellites, the fall of bodies on the surface of planets - so many phenomena can be described and calculated with Newton's law. Here is some regularity, some understanding of the world's arrangement. No wonder Newton spoke about the harmony of the cosmos originating in God's plan. It is easy to imagine Newton's excitement at his discovery of the universe's orderly arrangement.

Let me take an other example, showing the connection between the particular and the fundamental and illustrating the rationality

Chapter 2 — Order

in the world. We remember from school days the chart of chemical elements, called Mendeleev's periodic system. Mendeleev based this chart on regularities in the chemical and physical properties of chemical elements. Elements with similar behavior are placed in the same group. Similarities in chemical behavior can be related to the similarity in atomic electronic configurations. Wave mechanics describes these in terms of the waves of probabilities.

Atoms are not just haphazard assemblies of atomic nuclei (protons and neutrons) and electrons. There is a general principle in nature, related to the properties of a group of particles in the microworld, on which atomic electronic configurations depend, the so-called Pauli exclusion principle which expresses exclusion from an atomic system of those electrons which are in the same quantum state.

This principle shapes the electronic atomic configurations which then influence the chemical and physical properties of chemical elements. We can talk about a principle which influences all chemistry, at the same time rejecting reductionism. The Pauli principle also plays a role in the behavior of such substances as electrical conductors or insulators, and in the resistance of some stars to gravitational collapse. There again is a principle which, to a religious person, can mean an idea of how God arranged the world.

We shall later discuss an example of reductionism related to levels in the cosmic evolution: atoms, molecules, life. Clearly, life cannot be completely reduced to molecules and atoms. There is a connection between higher and lower levels in the cosmic evolution, but not complete dependence; evolution brings novelties.

I would like to add my own experience of grasping the connection between particular phenomena and basic principles. I think that probably just anyone who has done research has had such an awareness. It is sometimes quite overwhelming, speaking to us about a meaningful, orderly world, about God. At other times, the awareness is present but we do not think about it, being lost in details of research. Loud or quiet, it is always there, and without it no science makes sense.

I enjoyed studying physical chemistry and physics and my interest increased when I began laboratory research. My pleasure

SCIENCE AND FAITH

was clouded, however, by the thought that my subject, however fascinating, was still non-alive matter. Why, I asked myself, didn't I dedicate my life to the most important subject of all – the human soul? Did I choose to study science instead of theology because of opportunism and vanity? But then came the wonderful moment of my full awareness of the fundamental order in nature. I remember every detail of that moment. It was late afternoon. I was alone in the laboratory, investigating electrical arc plasma. My goal was to find the best plasma conditions to obtain the strongest intensities of atomic spectral lines of elements present in plasma as traces. I observed plasma temperature distribution, electron density distribution, mass and energy transport. These parameters are connected with some fundamental natural laws. I had thought a hundred times about the connection between the particular phenomena I investigated and fundamental laws, without getting excited;but that afternoon, the awareness of this connection overcame me so strongly : there is an orderly arrangement in nature and God acts everywhere; we only need to open our minds and our senses.

Later, I worked on the processes in arc plasma in collaboration with colleagues and many students. But I never had a moment of such strong emotion as the one I have described. There was, however, always some excitement when my thoughts made the connection between the particular and the fundamental, and this excitement was like a prayer of gratitude to God.

Some years afterwards, I collaborated with colleagues and students on plasma etching and deposition of organic polymers. In polymers, a pattern of chemical structures, of chemical bonding of several atomic groups, repeats itself many times. In deposition of polymers, gas plasma constituents, atoms and molecules, partly ionized, form a rather complex solid material. In the etching process, the solid material disappears; its atoms and molecules become parts of gas plasma.

In both cases, deposition or etching, the total entropy of the whole process, including the sustaining of plasma, will increase.

My colleagues and I could choose the experimental conditions such as gas composition and flow velocities, electrical plasma

Chapter 2 — Order

parameters to obtain deposition or etching. As in any scientific experiment, or any technological production, a small error can influence the co-ordination of all parts of the experiment and cause a fiasco. During the experiments, my thoughts wandered to the billion processes occurring every moment in nature. Every moment, billions of structures collapse but billions of new ones appear in an evolving universe: a wonderful, incredible co-ordination and coherence occurs in the cosmic evolution. Is it possible that nobody's will is behind the direction of cosmic evolution and coherence?

SCIENCE AND FAITH

EVOLVING UNIVERSE

The Universe, Its History and Its Future

Cosmology has brought an understanding that the universe had a *beginning*, at least in the form of stars and galaxies,
an *evolution*, and will have
an *end*, at least in the sense that no physical life in
any form at all will exist.

In 1948, George Gamow described the beginning and early moment of the universe. According to this "classical" Big Bang theory, the universe exploded into existence some 10-20 billion years ago. In the initial singularity matter was extremely hot and dense and the universe was very small. In a singularity, a ray of light and path of any particle will come to an end [71]. The Big Bang also meant the beginning of time and space. The universe is not created in time and space; time and space were instead created with the universe. The idea that time has not existed for ever but was created with the world was expressed by St. Augustine and based on theological reasoning. I shall later return to that.

A cosmological approach to the history of the universe is based on astronomy, on the general theory of relativity and other branches of physics, especially the physics of high energy particles. The discovery of the expansion of the universe, made by atomic spectroscopy in astro-physical research, contributed essentially to an understanding of the cosmic evolution. To-day's experimental study of collisions of particles accelerated to very high energies offers some information about the early, very hot universe.

SCIENCE AND FAITH

The early universe was probably in a state of almost perfect symmetry; and its history is about expansion, cooling, breaking the symmetries, differentiation, formation of new structures, increasing complexity.

We assume to-day that four fundamental forces exist in nature: gravity, electromagnetism, strong and weak nuclear forces. The strong nuclear force is related to the attraction of particles in atomic nuclei, e.g. it acts between neutron and proton, between proton and proton and between neutron and neutron. The weak nuclear force is related to radioactivity.

It is assumed that, immediately after the Big Bang, all the forces in nature were unified, as described by the Super Unified Theory. However, any discussion of processes at the earliest time of the universe encounters great difficulties. Theoretical work on the early universe generally searches for mathematically symmetrical solutions.

After 10^{-43} seconds at temperatures of about 10^{32} °K, gravity separated from other forces; unification of the three remaining forces is described by the Grand Unification Theory - GUT. At about 10^{-35} second after the Big Bang and temperatures of about 10^{28} °K, the strong nuclear force left the electroweak force, made up of the weak nuclear force and electromagnetism. Finally, at about 10^{-10} second (ten billionth part of the first second) and temperatures of about 10^{15} °K, the electroweak force divided into two; this marked the establishment of the four fundamental forces which we know to-day.

The distinction between particles in the very early universe, about 10^{-43} second, was unclear. It is assumed that particles called quarks and gluons (particles related to the connection between quarks) later existed along with the family of particles called leptons which include electrons and neutrinos. At the time of about 10^{-6} second (a microsecond) after the Big Bang, quarks formed neutrons and protons, constituents of atomic nuclei.

Energy can be transformed into matter and vice versa, as Einstein described in his famous equation $E = mc^2$. Two kinds of matter, matter and antimatter, can be created from energy. Matter and antimatter differ in their electrical charges and other qualities, but are similar in many properties. In principle, it is possible to

Chapter 3 — Evolving Universe

imagine a world of antimatter only, but not a world of matter and antimatter which do not "tolerate" each other. Their contact results in the anihilation of both and the creation of energy.

During parts of the first second after the Big Bang, opposite processes occurred: matter and antimatter were created from energy and were anihilated as they collided, producing radiation as a result. Because matter exceeded antimatter in the early universe, only matter remained after the first second.

A proton represents the nucleus of a hydrogen atom. The fusion of two protons and two neutrons leads to the formation of a helium nucleus He^4. Helium nuclei were formed about one minute after the Big Bang.

The ratio of protons to helium nuclei, approximately 3:1, was fixed in about the first minute. The abundance of hydrogen and helium in nature, found today, corresponds exactly to this ratio which, as we shall discuss later, was exceedingly important for the evolution of a universe in which life could exist. The strength of nuclear forces influenced first the ratio of protons to neutrons and then the ratio of protons to helium nuclei.

Before neutrons and protons, before nuclei, before atoms and molecules, before all the complex biochemistry, there existed fundamental forces in nature, natural laws and constants, which influenced the formation of species. As we believe to-day, these natural laws and constants have remained the same.

The initial conditions of the universe, natural laws and constants, paved the way for cosmic evolution. They enabled evolution to progress without determinism.

Almost a million years (300,000 - 1,000,000) passed before atoms were formed; and it took from a million to a billion years for the first galaxies to appear.

When the temperature decreased to several thousand °K, the interactions of protons and electrons led to the formation of neutral hydrogen atoms. Before that, at higher temperatures, neutral atoms were promptly ionized, e.g. the electrons separated by interaction with high energy photons.

The early stage of the universe was characterized by the coupling of matter and radiation. When matter won over antimatter

SCIENCE AND FAITH

in the process of anihilation, the existing photons were scattered by electrons. As the universe expanded, the density of electrons and protons, as yet incapable of forming stable neutral atoms, decreased and the scattering occurred less frequently. However, radiation and matter were still coupled. But when temperatures decreased sufficiently for neutral atoms to exist, there were far fewer electrically charged particles and so less scattering of photons. Matter and radiation then went their separate ways, and this period in the cosmic evolution is called the decoupling era. Radiation from that era, cooled in time, was discovered as a uniform, isotropic radiation, now in the microwave electromagnetic region. This discovery was made in 1965, but theoretically predicted in 1948, and it represented further strong experimental support for the Big Bang theory and for a holistic view of the universe. The universe is not the sum of its parts, but a whole.

With the formation of the galaxies, stars and planets, the first stage of the universe, often described as a "fire-ball", came to an end. Still the holistic character of the universe is there; although galaxies, stars and planets have their own history, they are still parts of one whole, of the universe and its evolution.

The evolution of the universe occurred in an extremely delicate balance between expansion and gravitation. If gravitation had been a little stronger, the early universe would have contracted, and there would have been no stars and galaxies. If gravitation had been a little weaker, matter would have dispersed in the universe and no stars and galaxies could have formed. This delicate balance can be expressed through the value of the gravitational constant in Newton's law. An extremely small difference in the existing constant would have shaped a universe in which life in any form might well have been impossible. Instead, the gravitational constant has had just the right value for evolution of the universe to proceed to life.

The formation of stars and everything else in the universe was and is only possible because of the balance of opposite forces. Gravitation penetrates throughout and cannot be escaped. From one point of view we may regard gravity as a creative force; celestial bodies could not be formed without it. However, if there were no forces to oppose it, matter would be continuously compressed,

Chapter 3 — Evolving Universe

enormous gravitational fields would open and black holes form. Stars and everything else in the universe exist because opposing forces, basically electromagnetic in origin, act against gravity. An inner heat pressure formed in stars due to nuclear fusion reactions also opposes gravity. The idea of opposite processes is important in understanding the temporary stability of different levels of the cosmic evolution.

After the "fire-ball" stage of the universe, the first stars were formed from the only materials which then existed, almost exclusively hydrogen and helium, plus very small amounts of lithium, and hydrogen and helium isotopes. How were the heavier elements formed? Cosmology tells us that they were created in the cores of stars.

The fusion of hydrogen nuclei first formed helium, then carbon, oxygen and many other elements. Carbon, oxygen, hydrogen, nitrogen are the main components of life on Earth. The formation of carbon and oxygen in a star's nuclear fusion reaction is once again a wonderful, precisely tuned performance.

Stars do not live forever. Hydrogen nuclei are exhausted in fusion reactions. Fusion reactions continue with helium and with heavier elements, but at the end instabilities cause an explosion of bigger stars, the so-called super-nova explosions. (Our bright sun is too small for that, and its fate will be different.) The heavier elements formed in the stars by nuclear fusion are pushed into cosmic space in a super-nova explosion by irradiated neutrinos. Elements heavier than iron can be produced by nuclear reactions with neutrons during the super-nova explosion; this is the so-called explosive nucleosynthesis. The cosmic material now consists not only of hydrogen and helium but also of heavier elements, and this will form the new generation of stars. Heavier elements are also constituents of our sun system, which means that it belongs at least to the second generation of stars. Indeed, our sun system was formed a mere 4.5 billion years ago. We cannot imagine any form of life developing from hydrogen and helium only;life evidently could not exist in the "fire-ball" stage of the universe. Neither could life exist before heavier elements formed in the core of the first generation of stars and the second generation came into being.

SCIENCE AND FAITH

During the "fire-ball" stage of the universe, the "life" of the first generation of stars and the time when new stars were formed, the universe expanded enormously.

Life began on Earth in the simplest forms, progressing to the more complex, culminating in the creation of humankind.

The "classical" Big Bang theory is in fair agreement with the results of experimental investigations into the abundance of elements in nature and the existence of cosmic background radiation. Still, the theory cannot explain all observable phenomena. In 1980, Alan Guth suggested a model which essentially represents a modified Big Bang theory, according to which an extremely rapid expansion occurred in the very early universe. This rapid expansion, called inflation, occurred during a very short period of time, 10^{-30}s. The inflation theory explained some observations, but other questions are still open. [72]

The newest development of ideas in the cosmology of the very early universe necessarily includes quantum physics to explain events. Now, not without difficulties, a new branch of physics is developing: quantum cosmology.

Although to-day's scientists have different approaches to happenings at the very beginning of the universe, there is general agreement about the expansion of the universe and the fact that we live in an evolving universe which now presents us with an enormous diversity of structures and orderly complexity.

What does cosmology predict for the future?

The energy which the sun radiates could remain fairly constant for the next 5,000 million years. As we have discussed, opposite processes in the sun - such as gravitation and thermal pressure due to nuclear reactions of fusion of hydrogen in its core – keep its shape. The sun magnificently radiates energy, most of which just represents an increase of entropy; the energy source is depleted and the irradiated energy cannot be used in the universe. But that is certainly not true for that part of the energy which reaches Earth. Life on Earth is possible because it receives the right amount of sunshine.

In about five thousand million years from now, all the sun's hydrogen will have disappeared in nuclear fusion reactions. The sun's core will shrink, its temperature will rise and fusion reaction

Chapter 3 — Evolving Universe

of helium will be ignited. The energy thereby released will not only change the sun's radiation but will enlarge its diameter, and it will become a "red giant", perhaps engulfing the Earth. When all the helium has been used up, the heavier elements will take their place as nuclear fuel, but relatively soon no more energy will be released. The sun will then contract to become as small, perhaps, as the Earth is now; and it will become a cold, dark "white dwarf". All this will lead to the end of any life in to-day's sun system.

The sun is now approximately in the middle of its existence as a stable star which radiates a fairly constant amount of energy. The sun had its beginning, then a period of relative stability, and it will come to an end; we can say that of everything else in the universe, and of the universe itself.

Cosmology does not exclude the possibility that the end of life on Earth could occur before the sun's drama unfolds. For example, there could be a collision with a comet arriving from cosmic space. But in the distant future, 5,000 million years away, the end seems to be inevitable. Before that, if human beings still exist, there is at least a possibility that they will escape our solar system to find a home elsewhere.

However, even this will not be a possibility in the more remote future. To-day, two models of the universe, open and closed, are chiefly discussed. The open model predicts that the universe will simply continue to expand; the closed model says that at a certain point, the universe will start to contract. With the expansion of the universe, individual stars will complete their cycles and "die", either in a super-nova explosion or by following a pattern similar to that of our sun. Gravity will continue to act. Entire galaxies will collapse into black holes and the matter escaping from them will be extremely cold and dark, its density very small. Eventually, the black holes will evaporate. Perhaps there will be some isolated radiation, perhaps some neutrinos. No physical life would be possible in any form. Even if the universe starts to contract at some point in the future, no life would be possible. In the case of a "closed" universe, the density of matter would increase with time, and perhaps a "fireball" stage would reform. If the universe starts to contract, entropy will not change its direction but continue to increase.

SCIENCE AND FAITH

The diagram in Fig 1. schematically describes the two models of the universe, open and closed .Our universe is very near the dividing line between them. If the universe had expanded too fast, galaxies and stars would never have formed;if too slowly, there would have been a big crunch before stars or even atoms had formed. We discussed this from the viewpoint of the very delicate balance between expansion and gravity. Whether the universe will follow the open or closed model depends, according to theory, on its total mass, unknown with sufficient precision to-day to come down on one side or the other.

Another idea is also indicated in Fig.1, although given disproportionally in relation to co-ordinates of the diagram. Physical life in any form could exist only in a time interval of the cosmic evolution, neither before nor after that.

Although the Christian religion's description of the end of the world is different to that of to-day's science, both predict an end.

It is improbable that the universe will repeat itself. There is a hypothetical theory of an oscillating universe. According to this, the universe is going through an infinite number of cycles of expansion, contraction to a new "singularity point", a state related to a new Big Bang, new expansion and so forth. Opponents predict that, for such an oscillating universe, the entropy per nuclear particle (ratio of the number of photons to the number of nuclear particles) would rise in every cycle. If our universe were the consequence of infinite pre-existing cycles, the entropy per nuclear particle would be infinite; this does not correspond to the facts.

Chapter 3 — Evolving Universe

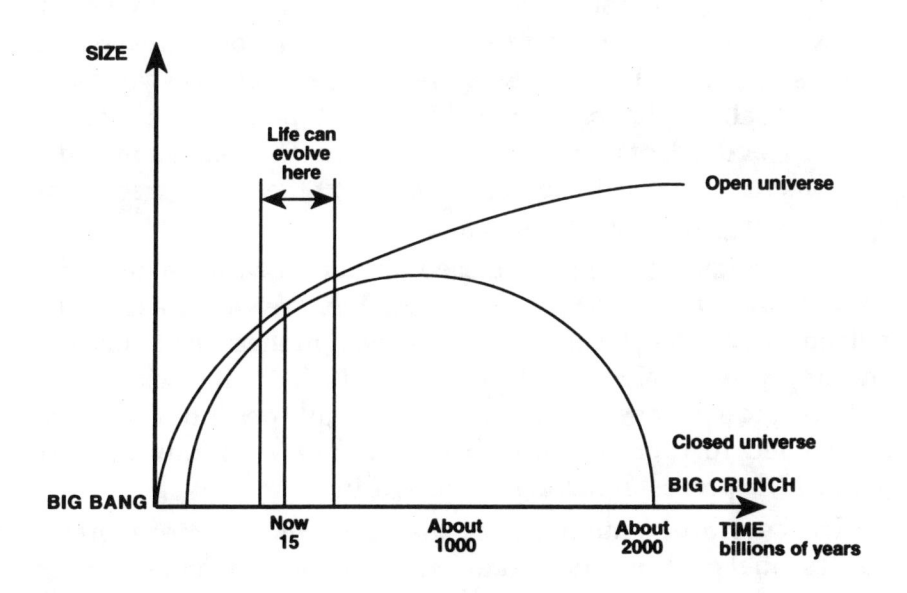

Fig.1. Diagram to illustrate:
a) the model of an open and a closed universe;
b) the idea that there is a time interval in the cosmic evolution in which eventually life could exist, but not before and not after.

We exist in a universe whose behavior is very close to the dividing line between these two models. If the universe had expanded too fast, galaxies and stars would never have formed; if too slowly, there would have been a big crunch before stars and even atoms had formed.

This diagram is based on a similar one in [73] and [74].

The divisions of the co-ordinates are not proportional.

47

SCIENCE AND FAITH

Two Opposite General Directions

The harmony and coherence in nature is not static. Matter changes constantly; this change is an essential quality of matter."Everything flows" as the Greeks put it. The changes we notice everywhere, on a large or small scale, using telescope or microscope [75]. The universe expands. We notice constant changes in the galaxies, in the stars, in nature around us, in every living cell; and we notice change in ourselves. We cannot stop or reverse the process of aging. The changes we notice are sometimes very slow and gradual, like the continental drift;sometimes they are dramatic like birth or death or a super-nova explosion. The changes in nature are sometimes cyclical like the seasons; but the cherry tree of this spring is not the same as last year's.

We can imagine an ideal closed system in which matter is in equilibrium and processes are reversible. We can calculate the outcome of chemical reactions for a system in thermal equilibrium and apply such calculations very usefully for many scientific or technological purposes. In this case we usually describe the system as "closed to thermal equilibrium"; but we know that the irreversible processes belong to our world.

Irreversibility means that the changes are more than a nonessential modification of one form of matter into another. There is an essential difference between the matter of this moment and the same matter of a previous one. Every moment corresponds to a smaller or bigger advance in cosmic evolution. Changes are related to time;irreversible changes express the fact that time is irreversible.

Where do the changes lead?

There are two opposite directions in nature, let us call them:

the general direction to life, and

the general direction to death.

Among the processes along a pessimistic arrow, along the general direction to death, we can think first about the spontaneous processes in nature which describe the thermodynamics function of entropy. There are mathematical expressions for entropy. The maximum value of entropy will be established spontaneously in closed systems. Entropy can relate to probability, less orderly states being more probable than more orderly ones. Processes in nature

Chapter 3 — Evolving Universe

spontaneously increase the disorder. There is a general tendency for differences between potentials in nature, sources of energy, to be diminished. If the concept of entropy is applied to the whole universe, there will be a tendency towards a state in which no activity or life could exist.

We have already seen that cosmological predictions for the distant future of our solar system and the whole universe are equally grim.

Biology tells us that different species have different life spans. This could be written in the genes, but for an individual, death always wins.

The existence of a general direction to life as a fundamental principle in nature is expressed (with some differences in interpretation) by many philosophers and scientists such as Bergson [76], Teilhard de Chardin [77], Walter Heitler [78], Holmes Rolston III [79], Paul Davies [80] and many others. This understanding is based on many observations and deep intuitive feeling.

Physicist **Paul Davies** writes:

Paul Davies is professor of Mathematical Physics at the university of Adelaide, Australia. He was previously professor of Theoretical Physics and Head of the Department of Theoretical Physics at the University of Newcastle, UK. He has written several books about science and religion. He has investigated quantum effects in the very early stage of the universe;he works on physics of complexity and foundations of quantum mechanics.

> **"There exists alongside the entropy arrow another arrow of time, equally fundamental and no less subtle in nature.... I refer to the fact that the universe is progressing - through the steady growth of structure, organization and complexity - to ever more developed and elaborate states of matter and energy... The progressive nature of the universe is an objective fact." [81]**

Davies and others talk about an "organizing principle in nature". There is an attempt to find a function which will express this organizing principle: something similar, but opposite, to entropy. There are suggestions that such a function should be related to complexity. Coherence and orderliness permeate the universe. However we also use "order" to describe a rigid system, such as a crystal. A dynamical coherence which is at the base of the general direction to life could perhaps be related to the "orderly complexity", but the idea seems deeper than our playing with words.

The history of the universe tells us about the growth of diversity and orderly complexity. The path of cosmic evolution proceeded in a very delicate balance of opposite forces. Despite the strong probability of a lifeless universe, a wonder occurred; evolution led from hot, dense plasma to galaxies, stars and planets, to a stage upon which life could develop. The evolution of life is also characterized by growth of diversity and orderly complexity.

With the creation of human beings, evolution assumed a new character. In human beings the essence of evolution is above all concerned with spirituality and love. The life of Jesus Christ on Earth, His teaching, death and resurrection, gave deep meaning to the evolution towards spirituality and love. I am convinced that the goal of the general direction to life is eternal spiritual life in love. Such a conviction is not only an expression of my faith and my feelings; to think differently, that the path of the cosmic evolution leads to nothing, would be quite unreasonable.

Two general directions advance simultaneously and irreversibly to opposite goals : life and death. Both are related to the notion of time in which a realization of the universe's potential occurs. The two general directions are connected. An increase in orderly complexity, an advance along the direction to life, occurs in the physical world only at the expense of an increase in total entropy.

Figs. 2 and 3 represent some ideas about the two general directions in nature. Fig. 3 expresses the idea that advance in the general direction to life occurs through many levels. We shall later discuss this figure.

Chapter 3 — Evolving Universe

REALIZATION OF THE POTENTIAL OF THE UNIVERSE. INCREASE IN ORDERLY COMPLEXITY.

General Direction to Life

time

DECREASE OF THE UNIVERSE'S POTENTIAL FOR EXISTENCE OF LIFE. DEGRADATION OF ENERGY. INCREASE OF ENTROPY.

General Direction to Death

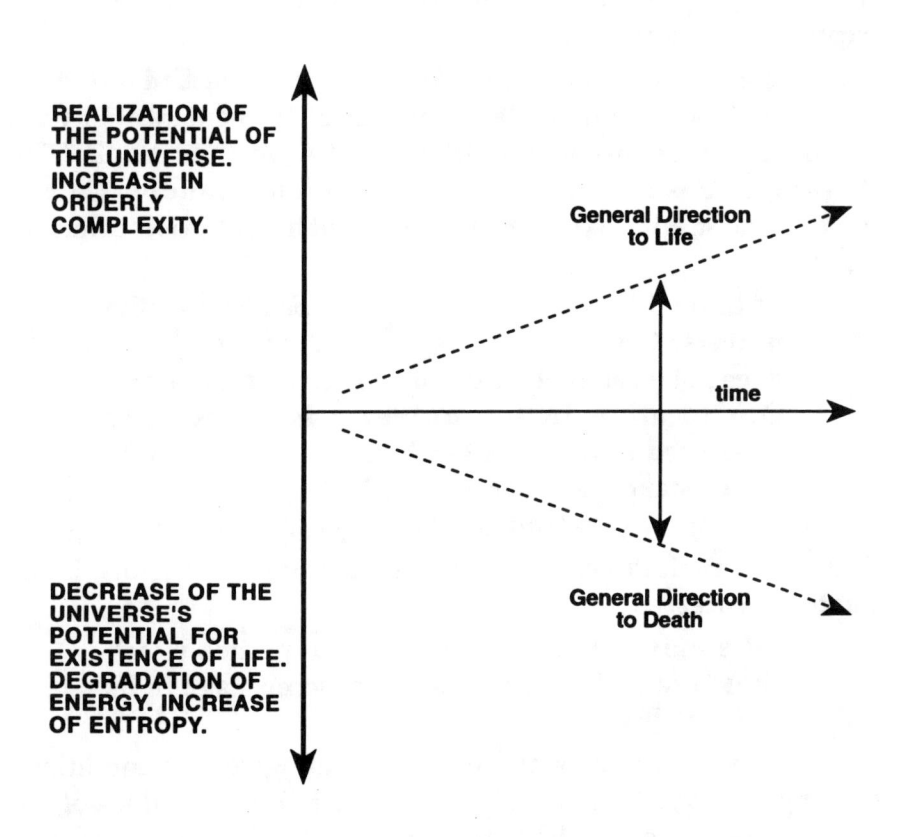

Fig.2. A sketch of two general directions of natural processes, to life and death. Both directions proceed irreversibly and both are related to the notion of time.

The two general directions are connected. Increase in orderly complexity occurs only at the expense of an increase in total entropy.

There is an uncertainty in to-day's physical description of the very early universe.

SCIENCE AND FAITH

The Anthropic Principle

The anthropic principle is formulated and discussed in depth by physicists; appealing as it is to theologians, they have not initiated discussions about it. There are some physicists who disagree with the anthropic principle and its theological implications, but many express their support.

John Barrow, professor of Astronomy at the University of Sussex, UK, and **Frank Tipler,** professor of Mathematical Physics at Tulane University, New Orleans, USA, in their book "The Anthropic Cosmological Principle", quote **Brandon Carter,** astrophysicist, who expressed an idea about the anthropic principle in 1974:

> **"Although we do not regard our position in the universe to be central or special in every way, this does not mean that it cannot be special in *any* way... Our location in the universe is necessarily privileged to the extent of being compatible with our existence as observers." [82]**

There are several definitions of this principle, one of which, the Strong Anthropic Principle (SAP), can be formulated (Barrow, Tipler quote **B. Carter**) as :

> **"The universe must have those properties which allow life to develop within it at some stage in its history". [83]**

The basic features of the universe were given by conditions existing very shortly after it began to expand. If the values of the physical constants, which fix the strength of the fundamental forces in nature, had been different by a small fraction of existing values, the universe would be one in which no life in any form could exist. Nobody can deny the existence of an astonishing number of coincidences which made life in the universe possible. In an article in the journal Nature, physicists **B. J. Carr** and **M. J. Rees** write:

> **"The basic features of galaxies, stars, planets and the everyday world are essentially determined by a few microphysical constants and by the effects of gravitation.....Several aspects of our universe - some**

Chapter 3 — Evolving Universe

of which seem to be prerequisites for the evolution of any form of life - depend rather delicately on apparent "coincidences" among the physical constants....The universe must be as big and diffuse as it is to last long enough to give rise to life." [84]

The question can be asked: why is there such an extremely fine tuning of physical constants, hence strength of physical forces in nature? Many facts indicate the answer: there is in nature the anthropic principle which directed the evolution of the universe towards life from its very beginning.

Let us discuss some examples of this fine tuning.

As mentioned, a balance existed from the beginning of the universe between its expansion and gravitational attraction. The Big Bang adjusted this balance in such a way that the universe just escaped its own gravity.

The ratio of protons to neutrons and protons to helium nuclei, established in the early universe, were essential for cosmic evolution to life. A small increase in the strength of the strong nuclear force would have caused an increase in the amount of helium. The material which existed in the "fire-ball" stage of the universe formed the stars. If less hydrogen had been used as the initial fuel for nuclear fusion reactions in the stars' cores, stars would have had shorter lives. The life of the sun would probably not have been long enough to enable life on Earth to evolve. In addition, hydrogen is a compound of water, a compound of organic life;without it life could not exist.

Sir Bernard Lovell, astronomer, wrote:

Sir Bernard Lovell is Professor Emeritus, University of Manchester, UK. He was previously Director of the Nuffield Radio Astronomy Laboratories. Several universities have given him honorary doctorates.

"... It is an astonishing reflection that at this critical early moment in the history of the universe, all of the hydrogen would have turned into helium if the force of attraction between protons - that is, the nuclei of the hydrogen atoms - had been only a few percent stronger. In the earliest stages of the expansion of the universe, the primeval condensate

> would have turned into helium. No galaxies, no stars, no life, would have emerged. It would have been a universe forever unknowable by living creatures. A remarkable and intimate relationship between man, the fundamental constants of nature and the initial moments of space and time seems to be an inescapable condition of our existence ... Human existence is itself entwined with the primeval state of the universe." [85]

The abundance and ratio of elements heavier than hydrogen and helium also had vital importance for the evolution of life on Earth. As we noted, these heavier elements were formed in the stars' cores through nuclear fusion reactions. Let us look at carbon and oxygen and the processes of their nucleosynthesis in the stars.

The first nuclear fusion reaction in a star's core was the fusion of hydrogen into helium, which leads to a decrease of hydrogen in the star and hence a decrease of its fusion reactions. Gravity then increases the core's density and its temperature rises to the point at which the fusion reactions of helium can be ignited. This scenario - exhaustion of a particular fuel, increase of core temperature, leading to the fusion of heavier nuclei - can be repeated several times.

From the biological point of view, the formation of carbon nuclei is extremely important.

There is a possibility of the forming of carbon nucleus C^{12} by the simultaneous fusion of three helium nuclei He^4; another important possibility is the first formation of the beryllium nucleus Be^8 by the fusion of two He^4 and then the fusion of beryllium with a third helium into carbon C^{12}. The probability of fusion reactions occurring, the so-called "reaction cross section", depends on the total energy of the reacting particles. For either fusion reactions leading to the formation of the nucleus C^{12}, the reaction cross section rises relatively slowly with the increasing energy of the particles. However, the reaction cross section suddenly rises to very high values for given particles' energies, implying a great probability that the fusion reaction occurs by the interaction of particles. These special values of the total energy of the particles, when the probability of fusion is very high, are related to the so-called nuclear resonance. If the total energy of particles is smaller or greater than values of nuclear resonance, the probability that the interaction will cause fusion is much less. The energy of particles depends on the temperature in the core of the stars. Well, those temperatures correspond precisely to the

Chapter 3 — Evolving Universe

nuclear resonance for fusion reactions which form the nucleus C^{12} and which go both ways, either in simultaneous interaction of three helium nuclei or with intermediate production of a beryllium nucleus. If the total energy of the reacting particles had not corresponded to the values of nuclear resonance for production of C^{12}, the amount of carbon produced in the star would have been too small, and carbon-based life in the universe would not exist.

The reaction of carbon synthesis via intermediate production of a Be^8 nucleus, has an important advantage over the simultaneous interaction of three He^4 nuclei, because only two particles react simultaneously. However, the nucleus Be^8 is unstable, and the formation of the carbon nucleus is sensitive to its "life time". The life of Be^8 should not be too short; it should exist long enough for interaction with the helium nucleus and formation of the carbon nucleus. If the life of Be^8 were too long, this could, for several reasons, influence nucleosynthesis in the stars and drastically decrease the possibility of life. Another "coincidence": the life span of the Be^8 nucleus is just right.

That is not the last of the "coincidences" related to carbon. Carbon C^{12} forms the oxygen nucleus O^{16} in the fusion reaction with one more helium nucleus. The formation of oxygen is important, but if too much oxygen were formed there would be insufficient carbon to support life. How much oxygen will form depends on the resonant energy of interacting particles, carbon and helium. The temperature in the stars' cores does not correspond to the resonant energy for fusion of carbon and helium into the oxygen nucleus. The probability that oxygen nuclei will form is not too high. As a result, carbon in the nuclear fusion reactions in the stars is not too depleted and there is enough carbon in nature. The relative abundance of carbon and oxygen in the universe is similar.

The values of particle energies which correspond to nuclear resonance in nuclear fusion reactions are related to nature's fundamental forces, especially the strong nuclear and electromagnetic force. We can say that if the strength of these forces were different, life in the universe would not exist.

Astronomer **Fred Hoyle** considered the "coincidences" related to the nuclear synthesis of carbon and oxygen so marvellous that, in talking about them, he used the expression a **"put-up-job"**. Regarding the positioning of the nuclear resonance, he wrote:

> **"If you wanted to produce carbon and oxygen in roughly equal quantities by stellar nucleosynthesis, these are the two levels you would have to fix, and your fixing would have to be just about where these levels are actually found to be ... A common sense**

SCIENCE AND FAITH

> interpretation of the facts suggests that a superintellect has monkeyed with physics, as well as chemistry and biology, and that there are no blind forces worth speaking about in nature." [86]

The "fine tuning" of the fundamental constants in nature can be seen in many examples. If the electric charge of the electron had been slightly different, chemistry of any kind would not exist.

Physicist **Freeman Dyson**:

> "Nature has been kinder to us than we had any right to expect. As we look out into the universe and identify the many accidents of physics and astronomy that have worked together to our benefit, it almost seems as if the universe must in some sense have known that we were coming." [87]

What Dyson and others tell us is that, at the beginning of time, in the hot, dense plasma, there existed already the prerequisites for life, perhaps not exactly the life we know, but life in general.

Physicist **Mike Corwin**:

> "This 20-billion year journey seems at first glance tortuous and convoluted, and our very existence appears to be the merest happenstance. On closer examination, however, we will see that quite the opposite is true - intelligent life seems predestined from the very beginning...Life as we conceive it demands severe constraints on the initial conditions of the universe....It is not that changes in the initial conditions would have changed the character of life, but rather that any significant change in the initial conditions would have ruled out the possibility of life evolving later....The universe would have evolved as a lifeless, unconscious entity. Yet here we are, alive and aware, in a universe with just the right ingredients for our existence." [88]

It is impossible not to be aware of many "coincidences", of the "fine tuning" of the universe from its very beginning, towards life. We can accept this awareness because it is impossible not to accept

Chapter 3 — Evolving Universe

it and not to think about the meaning of the facts. Or we can ask the question : is the universe telling us something?

George Wald, biochemist, said :

> "This universe is fit for it" (for life);"we can imagine others that would not be. Indeed this universe is only just fit for it....Sometimes it is as though nature were trying to tell us something, almost to shake us into listening." [89]

And **Mark Demianski,** cosmologist and astrophysicist:

> "Somebody had to tune it very precisely.
> The odds against a universe like ours emerging out of something like the Big Bang are enormous. I think there are clearly religious implications." [90]

Levels of Cosmic Evolution

Cosmic evolution is an undeniable fact. It does not occur in a smooth, uniform climb up the path in the general direction to life, Fig. 2, but through many levels, the lower ones contributing in different ways to the existence of the higher.

Each level has *a beginning, a duration* characterized by irreversibility, and *an end.* For its duration, each level can contribute to the general direction to life, and we may call this contribution *an achievement* which in fact it is.

Taking a holistic view, we can say that the duration of a level, like everything else, depends on everything in the universe. It depends on the initial conditions of the universe, on physical laws, on the values of physical constants, on the conditions of other objects in the universe at the observable level (for example, the sun and life on Earth), on the balance of all forces acting on the system, on variations exhibited by the system.

Let us observe the duration of a level with a model which sometimes represents only an idealization of a more complex reality, a model of the acting *opposite forces (opposite processes, opposite phenomena).* We mentioned such a model when discussing gravity, without which the universe would have been almost featureless.

SCIENCE AND FAITH

Gravity brings many objects into existence; however, they exist because of the simultaneous action of opposing forces.

A level's duration depends on the balance of opposite processes; for progress in the universe this balance is more important than the action of any one process or force.

The path of each level from beginning to end is irreversible. However, *the fact that the universe did evolve towards orderly complexity also means that the duration of each level was sufficiently long to permit achievement.*

All experience tells us that every level will end; and with apologies for using anthropomorphic terminology, we should not be sorry, but glad of the achievement. Each moment on a level is characterized by the inescapable approach to its end plus the possibility of achievement.

Fig. 3 gives examples of different levels :
a) the entire universe of galaxies, stars, planets;
b) the sun system;
c) life in general;
d) humanity.
e) the life of an individual human being is also shown to express an analogy between levels of the universe and human life.

We shall not describe in depth the duration of different levels, opposite processes and achievements, only point out some general ideas about each.

At level a, if talking about the model of opposite processes, we can observe expansion and gravitational attraction. We have already mentioned the delicate balance between these opposite processes which was "just right" for the development of the universe, allowing formation of atomic nuclei, atoms, molecules, galaxies, stars, planets, heavy elements in the stars' cores, the sun system and so forth.

The duration of the sun system, level b, is connected to the balance between gravitational attraction and pressure in the sun, relating to the nuclear fusion reaction of hydrogen into helium. Opposite processes account for the sun's relative stability. The sun's luminosity has changed by only 30 % during its "life"; and this

Chapter 3 — Evolving Universe

rather constant radiation, in terms of achievement, has made the evolution of life on Earth possible. The depletion of hydrogen, a fuel for nuclear fusion in the sun, is bringing the sun system closer to its end; so this end is related to a change in the balance of the action of opposite processes.

For levels c (life in general), d (humanity) and e (life of an individual human being), the balance of all processes relating to life may be expressed in the idea of life versus death. To take any part in biological evolution, an individual life should not be too short. Without death, however, biological evolution could not take place. The journey to the more complex, more developed, requires a balance between life and death.

As an achievement on level c, we may take the evolution of life; and on levels d and e, we think of improvements in the human condition, but first of spirituality and love, of a deeper understanding of God and nature, of eternal life.

Level e has patterns similar to all others: a beginning, duration with possibility of achievement and a physical end.

SCIENCE AND FAITH

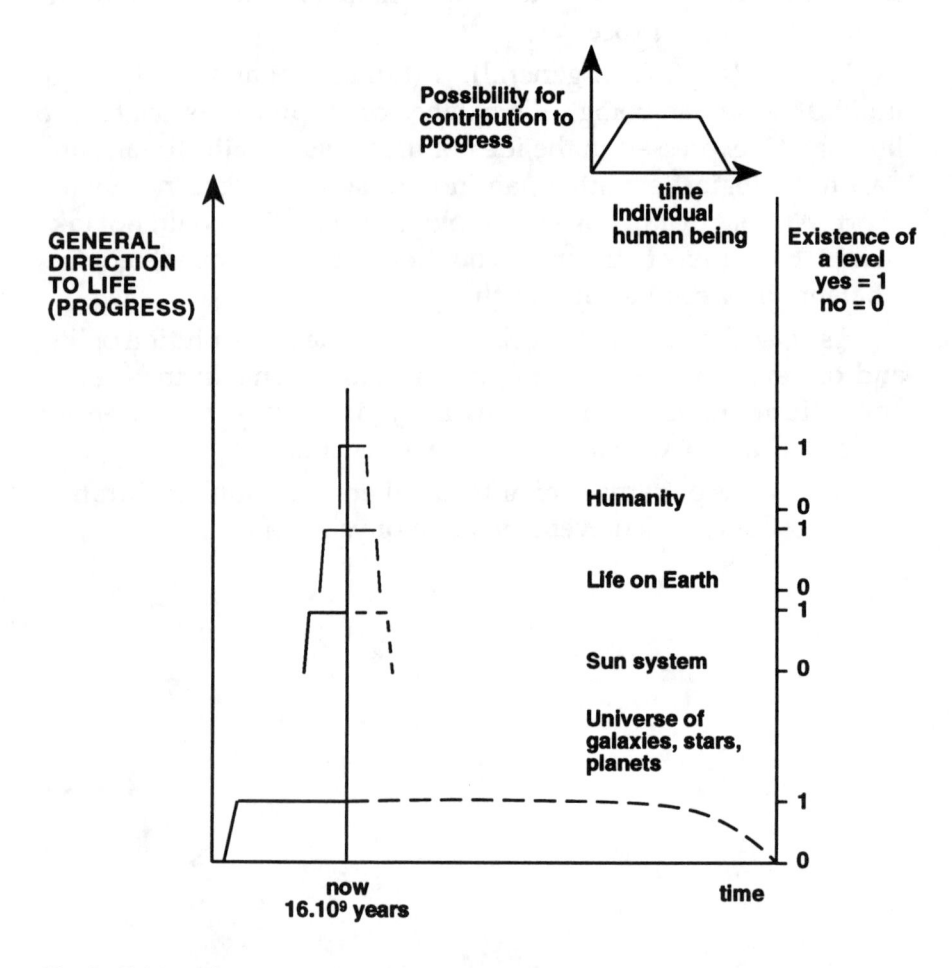

Fig. 3 Schematic presentation of some levels of the evolving universe. Each level has a beginning, a period during which it contributes to progress, and an end.

The predictions for the future of each level are given arbitrarily.

A separate diagram indicates the analogy between levels of the universe and the life of an individual human being.

Chapter 3 — Evolving Universe
"From Being to Becoming" and "Order Out of Chaos"

These are the titles of two books by **Ilya Prigogine;** the second one written with **Isabelle Stengers.** [91, 92]

"From Being to Becoming" stresses the meaning of the time arrow in physics, biology, human society. "Being" is related to the areas of science, such as Newton's physics, whose description of nature is time symmetrical in the past and future. "Becoming" is related to those fields where irreversibility and hence the time arrow play important roles, such as thermodynamics or "self-organization" in nature. The book connects these two fields.

"Order out of Chaos" confronts two irreversible directions in nature; one is expressed by the increase of entropy and disorder, the other by the increase of complexity and orderliness. Sometimes, an orderly system can rise spontaneously from one characterized by chaotic behavior.

Let us first explore the ideas of Prigogine and Stengers, as well as those systems which exhibit chaotic behavior.

First I would like to discuss the difference between a linear and non-linear system. Let us consider what happens when a stretching force acts upon a spiral system : the length of the spiral system increases and at the beginning the increase is linear;there is a direct ratio between force f and increase in the length d :

$d = a \times f$, a is a constant, a factor of proportionality.

Here, where the factor of proportionality is a constant, the system is linear. If the force f is two, three or four times greater, elongation d is also two, three, four times greater. In a linear system, the whole is the sum of its parts.

However, if we continue to increase the stretching force, we shall come to a region where the relation between force and elongation will no longer follow the simple equation above; factor a no longer is a constant. This can happen due to a change in the elasticity of the spiral, for example. Elongation d is no longer a linear function of f, and the system is now a non-linear one. In the non-linear system, the whole differs from the sum of its parts. The system cannot be analyzed under the assumption that it consists of subunits acting together. The resulting properties of the system could be unexpected.

If we increase the stretching force even further, the spiral will eventually break.

At the beginning of this century the mathematician and philosopher of science, Henri Poincaré, noticed an unpredictability between causes and

SCIENCE AND FAITH

effects in some systems where very small changes of the causes can have considerable changes in effects; and this was called chaotic behavior.

[It may be noted that in 1873, James Clerk Maxwell was invited to talk on the subject :"Does progress of science lead one to favour a belief in the existence of free will rather than determinism?" Maxwell there expressed the thought that infinitely small and uncertain variations in the present state can produce essential and uncertain changes in the future state of a system, thus undermining a deterministic description of events.] [93, 94]

Investigations of non-linear systems which exhibit chaotic behavior intensified about 60 years after Poincaré's work. There were several reasons for this. First, computers permit sensitive calculations of the dependence of many systems on extremely small changes of initial conditions. Second, investigation of turbulence: the flow of a liquid through a tube is smooth and featureless at a slow speed; at a higher speed, the flow becomes irregular and chaotic, entering the region of turbulence. Third, the continuation of Poincaré's work on some non-linear theories. [95]

The work of Ilya Prigogine and his collaborators on the formation of structures with a high level of organization from systems in the regions of chaotic behavior, was received with great interest.

A system can have many subunits which exhibit fluctuations. If the system is closed to thermal equilibrium, these fluctuations are subdued. Here, as we have seen, the temperature distribution of all particles is similar and the systems tend to reach the maximum value of entropy. However, it could happen that the system is driven to a far-from-equilibrium state by some forcing agency. For example, we can observe a system as a function of imposed temperature gradient, or some other physical parameter. In far-from-equilibrium conditions, a critical moment can be reached when a bifurcation occurs in the progress of the system. Instead of there being one path in the system's evolution as a function of the external forcing agency, there are now two possible paths. These paths, or one of them, could be non-stable, falling into chaos, or stable, representing systems with a higher level of organization and higher order. The system "chooses" where to go. At the bifurcation point, the amplified fluctuations could drive the system to a new stabilized state. In a farther evolution of the system, each path bifurcates; a two-fork system branches and forms four forks, then an eight-fork system rises and so on. A characteristic of chaotic systems is a succession of bifurcations. There is a universality in the behavior of different chaotic systems; there are some rules, some constants which describe behavior in all of them. Somehow, systems with chaotic behavior are not so chaotic after all! We can talk about "structured chaos" or use some other words to express the idea that the chaotic systems in a far-from-equilibrium state are different from the state of a system closed to equilibrium, approaching maximum entropy, with a kind of a "chaotic uniformity" which characterizes disorder.

Chapter 3 — Evolving Universe

Systems near the bifurcation points behave differently to other parts of the same systems, the difference being their unpredictability. It is impossible to predict which path, among many, the system will choose after bifurcation. In a system's evolution, stable regions characterized by deterministic behavior are replaced by regions with chaotic behavior close to the bifurcation point. After bifurcation, there are again regions of deterministic probabilities, and later regions of unpredictability. Nature thus has a complex, pluralistic character with an interplay of necessity and chance.

It is necessary to understand what kind of unpredictability there is in a system which exhibits chaotic behavior. The essence of unpredictability, which non-linear systems could show, is related to the system's enormous sensitivity to initial conditions.

An infinitesimal change in initial conditions brings the appearance of different forms. Theories of a chaotic system do not in principle abolish Newton's deterministic ideas. Determinism, the causality, still exists but, despite that, the character of non-determinism prevails because of extremely high dependence on initial conditions. How precisely can we know the initial conditions? Ask, instead, how exactly the initial conditions can be given. First, the description always contains an error. The propagation of that error in time in the systems with chaotic behavior is not linear but exponential. But the question of unpredictability is even deeper than that. We can imagine that the knowledge of initial conditions should include the Brownian movement. As previously mentioned, this represents the movement of small pieces of material in liquid, caused by their collision with the liquid's molecules. This movement was first observed by Robert Brown who saw the typical zigzag motions in a random pattern through a microscope. Einstein expressed the quantitative theory of the Brownian movement. What if the initial conditions depended on quantum phenomena in the world of microphysics where Heisenberg's uncertainty principle has a role? The limit of predictability of the chaotic systems now represents not only the practical question but also a fundamental one.

Awareness of the system's enormous sensitivity to initial conditions came to expression in computer modeling of weather forecasting. Non-linear equations which must be used in this modeling led to such complexity that long term forecasting is practically impossible. The extreme sensitivity to initial conditions indicated that the smallest change in the circulatory pattern of the atmosphere might influence the weather. This is sometimes called the "butterfly effect"; half-jokingly, it is said that a mere flutter of a butterfly's wings to-day in Beijing can cause a storm next month in New York.

The possibility that chaotic behavior of a system can lead to structures of a higher level of organization is regarded by Ilya Prigogine and his coworkers as a fundamental organizing principle in nature. A new orderly system has to be *open* and have a *dissipative structure*. If it were closed it would soon degenerate, according to the second law of thermodynamics. *An open system imports energy from the surroundings and dissipates energy in the surroundings or, in other words, exports entropy into the surroundings.* Energy is continually dissipated into the surroundings;without a sufficient supply of energy from the surroundings, the system cannot exist. *The entropy of the surroundings* (the total entropy of the universe) *is continually increasing, but the dissipative structures maintain their coherence, their order, and can even increase the level of orderliness. The evolutionary processes of the universe advance at the expense of an increase of entropy.* Or, using our terminologies :the general direction to life (increase of complexity) develops together with the general direction to death (increase of entropy).

Coherent dissipative structures play an important role in the world in which we live, a world which is coherent and where the processes are mainly irreversible and mainly occur under non-equilibrium conditions.

Dissipative structures have a holistic character. Every molecule in a dissipative system behaves as if it "knows" about the state of the system as a whole, as if the long-range forces are acting in macroscopic regions. The molecular forces actually have a short domain of action, about 10^{-8} cm. Here are some examples of self-organization, when an orderly system spontaneously rises from one which behaves chaotically.

Heat moving evenly through a liquid suddenly transforms itself into a convection current; such a phenomenon occurs in nature but could also do so in any kitchen with a pot of water on the stove. The layer at the bottom is hotter, hence less dense; and the less dense layer tends to move upwards because of the temperature difference between the bottom and upper layers. However, if the temperature difference is small, the liquid's movement upward is subdued by viscosity. The convection current starts when a threshold is reached. If the conditions are carefully chosen, a stable flow is established, and millions of molecules suddenly form themselves into cells with a hexagonal structure or into rolls. Spatial patterns of a long-range order are established. These orderly patterns could be destroyed by further heating. As another example of a dissipative system which shows self-organization, there is what Prigogine called a "chemical clock". Reactions in this system are known as Belousov-Zhabotinsky reactions. A "chemical clock" represents a mixture of Ce (cerium) salts with some other chemicals, including some dyes sensitive to the valence degree of Ce ions. (Red for an excess of Ce^{3+} three valence ions, blue for an excess of four valence ions Ce^{4+}.) When the system is far-from-equilibrium, there can be an abrupt and periodic change of color. At one moment the system is blue, then red, then again blue and so forth. The changes occur at regular intervals. This is a coherent process involving billions of molecules;the system reacts as a whole. As Prigogine pointed out, to change color all at once, the molecules must be able to

Chapter 3 — Evolving Universe

"communicate". The energy must be supplied continually to the system which dissipates it back into the environment.

Let us take one more example from astronomy, often given in the literature : the famous red spot of Jupiter, known for keeping its shape for centuries. This spot is caused by the eddying motion of gases at Jupiter's surface. A computer simulation indicates that any particular element of fluid in the vicinity of the red spot behaves chaotically, hence unpredictably. Nevertheless the gases arrange themselves into a stable structure, coherent and rather consistent.

Life represents an open system, far-from-equilibrium. Living beings are not in an equilibrium with their surroundings. They take food, an organized form of energy, and radiate heat to the environment, thus dissipating energy; they import energy and export entropy. From the point of view of the second law of thermodynamics, there is degradation of energy. Prigogine and others supposed that living beings are able to "jump" suddenly to a higher level of organization, a process which can occur in systems far-from-equilibrium. These processes of self-organization should hence play an important role, possibly representing the first necessary changes in the steps of evolution, not gene mutation as suggested by Darwin.

Prigogine's ideas are not completely developed yet;one feels that there has been a deep intuitive grasp of natural processes, and very good points have been made, but the theory is not completely rounded out. Prigogine's idea stresses cosmic evolution. Ilya Prigogine, Nobel prize for work on thermodynamics of non-equilibrium systems :

"The concept of evolution seems to be central to our understanding of the physical universe." [96]

Prigogine and Stengers contribute to an understanding of the general direction to life. Both general directions, to life and to death (using our terminology) are closely connected. Under non-equilibrium conditions, orderly, more complex structures might spontaneously arise with the increase of entropy. An open system can import energy to form dissipative structures and to export entropy into the surroundings. In that way, entropy can produce order, not only express the degeneration of the existing one. Some structures in nature disappear, but others may arise. The universe has a pluralistic character. One other aspect of this pluralistic character is the interplay of necessity and chance. The universe is open to novelties; irreversibility plays an important role.

SCIENCE AND FAITH

"They" (irreversible processes) " are at the basis of important coherent processes that appear with particular clarity on the biological level." [97]

The ideas of Prigogine and Stengers consequently include a holistic view of the world. New orderly structures which appear in the self-organizing processes in nature cannot be reduced completely to the properties of previous ones.

Holism, Novelty, Reductionism

A holistic view and reductionism are both present in our understanding of nature. Reductionism considers that things in nature can be analyzed as a collection of individual parts of the system;in a universe evolving to more orderly complexity, reductionism attempts to describe an evolutionary level with the properties of lower, less complex levels. It is partly true that a higher level of complexity does not ignore lower levels. However, new qualities originate with rising complexity, novelties which cannot be reduced completely to the behavior of previous levels. In observing a system as a whole, we often find that it is more than the sum of the parts of which it consists. Let us observe the sequence of atoms, molecules, living beings. We have already discussed the Pauli exclusion principle which influences electronic atomic configurations; these are responsible for the behavior of the chemical elements and so are at the base of the coherence which chemistry exhibits.

However, the chemical behavior of molecules, e.g. chemical compounds, cannot be reduced completely to atomic behavior. It is clear to every chemist that the modes of chemical bonding of atoms in molecules, influenced by atomic electronic configurations, bring different molecular properties.

Let us observe chemical isotopes which consist of the same kind of atoms and the same number of each kind, yet still behave differently. The atoms in molecules are bonded in different configurations. For example, ethanol (ethyl alcohol) and dimethyl ether, consist of 2 carbon atoms, 6 hydrogen and 1 oxygen. Both have the formula C_2H_6O but they are very different;ethanol is used in beverages, dimethyl ether as a refrigerant.

Chapter 3 — Evolving Universe

Some chemical compounds can have the same numbers of atoms and even a rather similar atomic configuration, differing only in that one is a mirror-image of the other. They are chemical isomers. The small difference in the structure is sufficient to account for different behavior. For example, the metabolic processes in living organisms can depend on the kind of isomers taken as food or drugs;the body consumes one isomer, but not its mirror-image.

When we come to living beings, it is plain that total reductionism cannot be applied. Can we explain the behavior of any living thing by relating the amounts and properties of chemical elements, such as carbon, hydrogen, oxygen and others, of which it consists? There is some connection between the living being and its constituent elements, but it is evidently something very different, something unique. It is also evident that any living organism is much more than the sum of its parts, more than its roots and leaves, or in the case of an animal, more than its nose and paws. The whole complexity forms something unique, and only in this uniqueness does any part of the organism make sense.

The holistic character of an artistic creation is also self-evident. A painting is related to the materials used by the artist, but the painting is more than the sum of oils and canvas. We can similarly say that anything which we create to serve a purpose is not just the sum of its parts. Let us say that we plan to build a house and go to the brickyard. Here we can certainly accept the fact that a pile of bricks is just a cluster of individual ones. A pile of bricks is the sum of its parts. However, when we build a house from bricks and other materials, it is a new entity, not just the sum of its parts. The house needs coherence to exist and to be used for living. The same may be said about a machine we build; synchronization of all its parts is necessary, and the more sophisticated it is, the more synchronization it requires.

The holistic character is strong in all that God created on the path of the general direction to life, all that has purpose, and becomes more orderly, more complex. The opposite takes place on the path of the general direction to death;losing its purpose, orderly complexity and individuality, everything gradually loses its holistic character.

Earth is not only the sum of its parts, not merely a group of continents and water. Cosmology gives us a holistic view of the universe. Discoveries of the universe's expansion and cosmic background radiation speak of it as a whole with a common destiny. The general theory of gravity stresses the interconnection of everything in the universe. The time-space entity depends on the entire mass of the universe and influences the motion of all masses. We belong to Earth and to the whole universe.

Prigogine's ideas about cosmic evolution and novelties which have a system of organization higher than that found in lower systems are clearly opposed to reductionism.

A holistic view does not exclude reductionism. Linear and non-linear phenomena co-exist in our dynamic, evolving universe, complementing each other.

Necessity and Chance; the Idea of Opposites

There would not be a meaningful universe containing life without a fundamental order. We partly understand the existence of order in nature through physical laws. However, chance also plays a role in the cosmic evolution and is part of the design; it does not refute nature's fundamental order but, to the contrary, is part of it. Coherence in nature is more subtle than we imagine at first glance. How does the apparent determinism of physical laws blend with non-deterministic behavior and unpredictability? How do the opposites co-exist?

The introduction of statistics gave classical physics an understanding of how compatible deterministic and non-deterministic behaviors are. We can, for instance, observe the air temperature in a room which, measured by a simple thermometer, expresses the average energy of the air's molecules. There are also molecules with lower and higher energies, far from the mean value; there is an energy distribution. To some extent, individual molecules show the unpredictability of their energy with predictability belonging to the average behavior of the group.

Fundamentally, descriptions in statistical physics are only valid for an assembly of a great number of individual parts. As we discussed, the notion of entropy has a statistical character and can be applied only to large numbers of particles.

Chapter 3 — Evolving Universe

We speak now of thermodynamics; it is true that in everyday language we use the word " entropy" to express deterioration;we talk about the increasing entropy of a neglected house, or the entropy of the aging process of our bodies.

We often use statistics in our observation of events among a group of living beings. We talk about the age-span of a given species, thinking of an average life and knowing that individual lives may be shorter or longer.

Quantum mechanics offers another approach to non-deterministic phenomena. The uncertainty which the Heisenberg principle describes is an intrinsic characteristic of objects in the micro-world. We describe an atom with a wave function which can give, for the system as a whole, the distribution of the probabilities of electron densities. The iron grasp of determinism is just not valid in the micro-world.

The theory of Prigogine and his co-workers, as we saw, abandons the idea that only determinism and predictability determine happenings in the macro-world. The future brings novelties and cannot be completely reduced to previous levels of existence. The future brings advancement.

Neither the quantum theory nor Prigogine give any support at all to the idea that chaos rules the world. Order and coherence rule, a coherence which permeates everything and which is wonderful beyond description. According to Prigogine the cosmic evolution progresses in an interplay of chance and necessity.

The role of chance is sometimes described by an analogy to lock and keys. Imagine that we have many different keys with which we try, at random, to open a lock. One key out of many will open the lock and with that open the door to the next stage of progress. [98]

The interplay of necessity and chance and their roles in the cosmic evolution could also be expressed slightly differently. We discussed a model of cosmic evolution realized through many levels, each level having a beginning, an existence during which an achievement, a contribution to evolution, may occur, and an end. Achievement is not something which must happen in a deterministic way; it has no absolute necessity, necessity "per se"; yet it is more than a consequence. We shall return to this idea when discussing the idea of contingency.

SCIENCE AND FAITH

The idea that achievement is more than a consequence is easiest to accept when talking about human beings and free will. However, following Prigogine's ideas again, nature generally shows both deterministic and non-deterministic behavior.

The word "achievement" is perhaps one of the key words in this world. If God had created a perfect world at the beginning, the perfect people who inhabited it would have had no individuality. In the beginning God created potential and different modes for its realization which brought life, spirituality and love.

From **Arthur Peacocke,** biochemist and theologian :

Arthur Peacocke retired in 1988 from his post as Director of the Ian Ramsey Centre, Oxford, UK. Prior to this he was Dean of Clare College, Cambridge, UK. He is hon. D.Sc. De Pauw University, Indiana, USA, and he has been Warden of the Society of Ordained Scientists.

"......The full gamut of the potentialities of living matter could only be explored through the agency of rapid and frequent randomization which is possible at the molecular level of the DNA. Indeed the role of chance is what one would expect if the universe were so constituted that all the potential forms of organization of matter (both living and not-living) which it contains might be explored.

.... The original primeval cloud of fundamental particles at the "hot big bang" must have had the *potentiality* of being able to develop into the complex molecular forms we call modern biological life. It is this that I find significant about the emergence of life in the universe; the role of chance is simply what is required if all the potentialities of the universe are going to be elicted effectively.... Studies (of Prigogine and Eigen and their collaborators) demonstrate that *the mutual interplay of chance and law (necessity or determinism) is creative,* for it is the combination of the two which allows new forms to emerge and evolve.

It now appears that the universe has potentialities which are becoming actualized by the joint

Chapter 3 — Evolving Universe

operation in time of random, time-dependent processes in a frame-work of law-like properties...." [99]

Necessity and chance appear to be opposites; however, only in the presence of both does the cosmic evolution occur. Words may appear to exclude opposites but reality combines them.

The world is not rigid; rigidity could exist only in a world of deterministic necessity. The world is not chaotic; it would be chaotic if only chance ruled. The cosmic evolution in general and the evolution of life as part of it takes place in our universe where necessity and chance complement each other. We have already spoken of how balances were arranged with incredible delicacy so that the universe we know might appear and exist. The picture of a small, narrow path in the mountains, as an analogy for the possibility of cosmic evolution, confronts us again, this time with the emphasis on the complementarity of necessity and chance. *As a narrow mountain path between many abysses, including abysses of chaos and deterministic rigidity, led cosmic evolution to life, so does life continue to advance in many innovative ways.*

To summarize the idea of opposites:

There are two opposite general directions in nature. In the physical world, the advance in the general direction to life proceeds along with the advance in the general direction to death. Without an increase in total entropy, no orderly structures could be formed.

Achievement does not occur in some kind of vacuum, but in the presence of a tendency towards disorder and non-achievement; the achievement at each level of the universe's existence occurs simultaneously with that level's approach to its end.

The balance of opposite forces at each level of the universe maintains it and allows time for achievement; without this no evolution would take place.

Reductionism and holism appear to be opposite but are actually complementary.

What appear to be opposite, like chance and necessity, really support each other; they are of the same essence, the same design of the fundamental orderly arrangement in a dynamic, evolving universe.

SCIENCE AND FAITH

The root of this idea of opposite processes in nature appears in all the major religions and cultures;it is in Newton's law of mechanics and in the words of Heraclitus:

> **"Opposition unites. From what draws apart results the most beautiful harmony. All things take place through strife." [100]**

Life

Regardless of how we understand and interpret biological processes, we understand through our intuition, mind and feelings that life is opposite to death. Only after physical death does the second law of thermodynamics come fully to expression. Then there is nothing to maintain the marvellous coherence of a live organism, nothing to withstand increasing entropy.

Life is a complete novelty in the cosmic evolution. It cannot be reduced to chemistry, only to processes of inanimate matter. (For life, Walter Heitler uses the German word : *ein Urphänomen*.) [101]

Any form of life is a wondrous example of coherence and complexity; it exhibits a marvellous co-ordination of innumerable parts and processes. Even a simple cell reveals many interconnected chemical reactions. Everything serves to sustain the living organism as a whole.

To have a little more "flavor" about the complexity of living organisms, let us read from Andrew Miller, molecular biologist. He wrote a chapter "Biology and Belief" in "Real Science, Real Faith". [102] **Andrew Miller** was professor of biochemistry at Edinburgh University, UK, and is now head of the European Molecular Biology Laboratory, Grenoble, France.

> "In all living organisms there are three kinds of large molecules or macromolecules...These are the proteins, the nucleic acids and the polysacharides...Each of these three macromolecular types are long chain polymers composed of linear strings of smaller molecules called monomers, which act as subunits. These molecules all consist of only a few different chemical elements - carbon, hydrogen, oxygen, nitrogen and phosphorus and somewhat less of several other elements. .... Proteins are polymers of amino-acids. There are some twenty different kinds of amino-acids with differing size and electrical properties. It is the order in which these

Chapter 3 — Evolving Universe

different amino-acids occur along the protein chain which defines first how the protein molecule folds up to form a well defined three-dimensional structure and second, how that well defined structure is able to perform the specific function - enzyme, transport, light-harvesting, etc - of the protein in the organism. .... Structural molecular biology shows that living things function at the molecular level by a precise molecular positioning in space and high degree of synchronization in time. This accuracy of positioning in space and time is crucial for a single event like enzyme action, but within the cells of plants and animals millions of such events must further be orchestrated in space and time so that the whole cell functions properly, and of course the cell plays a defined role in a specific tissue (liver, brain, muscle, etc) which in turn has its specific role in the organism." [102]

In this chapter **Andrew Miller** discusses the difference between theism and atheism:

"When we try to clearly indicate the difference between theism and atheism the fundamental question is whether or not the universe has a purpose. Does the universe have a personal Creator and hence a purpose or is it entirely the result of mindless forces?

At the end he concludes:

"On the basis of these criteria" (of the world of **"coherence, fruitfulness, comprehensiveness, adequacy and intelligibility as well") and in the light of contemporary biology, belief in God is reasonable."** [103]

The functional, extremely complex biological order of a living organism is evidently very far from a state of maximum entropy and disorder into which, according to the second law of thermodynamics, a closed system evolves. Cosmic evolution evidently advances not only in the general direction to death but also in the general direction to life.

In each seed of a plant there is a blueprint of its future form, genetic characteristics for all species, and the organism battles to fulfill the plan. Think only about an organism's complicated healing process when injury occurs. But there is no complete uniformity

SCIENCE AND FAITH

within a species; one dandelion resembles another, but some details vary and some individuality breaks through. The more advanced life forms have more individuality.

According to Darwin, evolution of life is related to the random mutation of genes and natural selection. The second step, natural selection or survival of the fittest, does not necessarily mean that the stronger devour the weaker. Survival of the fittest might mean a better adaptation to the environment or some novelty in behavior.

The development of science will show whether or not evolution of life proceeds only according to Darwin's theory. Perhaps this theory indicates only some possibilities of the evolutionary process and other "mechanisms" will also be discovered. Instead of gene mutation as a first step, I. Prigogine and his collaborators suggested the creation of new, dissipative structures, creations of orderly systems in far-from-equilibrium conditions. Perhaps an increase in orderly complexity will be accepted as a fundamental principle in nature promoting the evolution of life.

For many people, myself included, God is the creator, whatever methods He uses along the general direction to life and however long He wants to take. God is the creator also in the sense of His permanent activity in the world. Progress as a result of an interplay of necessity and chance occurs because of God's arrangement and guidance.

Life came in the cosmic evolution when conditions were ripe for it. As indicated in Fig. 1, life could exist only during a given time interval of the evolution, neither before nor very probably after. Here the understanding is of life in any form. Even if we think about the possibility of life existing in forms different to those we know, our imagination should have a limit. The conditions for life to exist are precarious.

The universe expanded enormously while heavier elements formed in the stars' cores. As mentioned, without the enormous universe with its billions of galaxies and immense distances between them, life could exist nowhere.

The place where life could exist is also subject to specific demands. Earth has a solid crust; most material in the universe

Chapter 3 — Evolving Universe

probably consists of gas clouds or plasma balls. The Earth orbits around a star which has long been stable and radiates a relatively constant amount of energy to Earth. Earth's temperatures are not too low and not too high, but just about right for life to prosper.

In the history of the Earth the primordial atmosphere, if it ever existed, has been lost. It could have come through gases from solar nebula, by the release of gases from the planetary warmings after meteorites fell on its surface or by other processes. Before life started, a small amount of oxygen probably came through the processes of inorganic photochemistry. However, the most oxygen, O_2 molecules, important ingredients of life, developed through photosynthesis along with the evolution of life. O_2 molecules are also the precursors of atmospheric ozone O_3; the ozone layer was built in the atmosphere and protected life on the Earth from the sun's UV radiation. Many complicated processes and delicate balances, which atmospheric chemistry is still trying to understand, shared in creation of the Earth's atmosphere, disposed towards life. [104]

On two neighboring planets, Mars and Venus, each with a solid crust, dissimilar processes occurred in atmospheric development. These planets are very probably inhospitable to life because of their surface temperatures, among other factors. Because of the smaller mass and weaker gravity, many gases escaped from Mars. The Earth is indeed very special, not because of its size; Earth is only a grain of dust in the universe. Nor is Earth at the center of the universe; it is unlikely that a center exists. Earth is special because of its life which gave human beings a possibility for spiritual development and for what is most valuable: love. (See Brandon Carter's quotation [82] p. 52.)

We observed the general characteristics of life: an emphasized holistic essence of being, a wonderful co-ordination, a resistance to the increase of entropy, the existence of a plan, coded in DNA molecules, which comes to fruition through growth. Many other qualities appeared in the evolution of life.

A plant has a vegetative life, a direction and cycles of development. Animal life brings new properties. Senses are developed. The circle of interaction between animals and their surroundings is wider because of their mobility, and their ability to

SCIENCE AND FAITH

communicate is much greater. Some species, like bees or ants, have a fascinating ability to organize. Animals feel joy and sorrow; they have intelligence. Individuality is expressed more strongly. Instinct and learning determine animal behavior to a large extent.

Human beings differ totally from everything else in nature. They are also *"ein Urphänomen"*. Their distinction is less physical than spiritual. Beyond an ability to speak, beyond intelligence, their free will to choose between good and evil, to have a conscience, capacity for love, makes humans different from other life forms.

A Persian poet wrote:

> **"God sleeps in the mineral, dreams in the vegetable, stirs in the animal and awakens in the man."** [105]

Life is not an accident but a part of cosmic evolution.

God and Evolution of the Universe

The universe has not existed for ever, according to the Bible; at some point it was created by God.

Creation occurred gradually. God first created the conditions for life, then life itself in forms of increasing complexity, culminating in human kind. God's seven days of creation to which the Bible refers have nothing to do with our idea of a week.

> **" Do not ignore this one fact, beloved, that with the Lord one day is as a thousand years, and a thousand years as one day."** (Peter's Epistle II, 3/8) [2]

Victor Weisskopf, theoretical physicist, concludes his article "The origin of the Universe" :

> **"The origin of the universe can be talked about not only in scientific terms, but also in poetic and spiritual language, an approach that is complementary to the scientific one. Indeed, the Judeo-Christian tradition describes the beginning of the world in a way that is surprisingly similar to the scientific model."** [106]

And from the biologist and researcher **Alan Hayward,** on the subject of Genesis :

Chapter 3 — Evolving Universe

> "Many thousands of scientists today find no difficulty in accepting that simple, dignified account of creation. If geologists were to make a short cine film of the earth's history, as seen through the eyes of an imaginary observer on earth, Genesis 1 would provide quite a good summary of the film." [107]

Physicist **Semiramis Dionysiou-Kouimtzi**, professor of physics at the University of Thessaloniki, Greece, like many scientists, feels a deep connection between scientific and religious understanding of the truth. She writes:

> "The idea of evolution is predicted in the Old Testament. The formation of the universe is described in very simple terms and .... in Genesis are included the concepts of matter, motion and energy. It does not contradict Newton's laws of gravity nor Einstein's ideas.
>
> I believe the more accurate and delicate measurements we make the more we feel need of a mighty Creator.
>
> Without the knowledge of God, true knowledge is impossible." [108]

Robert Boyd, professor of physics, University of London and director of the Mullard Space Science Laboratory, a well known space scientist, stresses in his writing that the most distinctive attribute of God is love. About cosmic evolution he says:

> "I can only in honesty assert that I see the whole process from Big Bang (or even from an endless succession of expansions and contractions) to the occurrence of homo religiensis as wholly natural and as, in principle, a proper realm for humble scientific study. But equally, more importantly and, I believe, biblically, I see the whole process from beginning to end as the Act of God." [109]

Teilhard de Chardin is convinced that **God is Alpha and Omega;** God is the cause of the cosmic evolution and this evolution

SCIENCE AND FAITH

leads to Him. Between the beginning Alpha, and the end, Omega, there is ongoing time. With time, opposite universal processes develop, increasing entropy as a divergence, and increasing complexity as a convergence.

Paleontologist and monk, Pierre Teilhard de Chardin (1881-1955), describes a theory of cosmic evolution which includes the Darwinian theory of evolution of life and gives it a religious meaning. He describes first the evolution of matter, calling it cosmogenesis, then the evolution of life - biogenesis, and of society - noogenesis; Jesus Christ initiated evolutions's final phase - Christogenesis. He saw it all as an evolution to God.

In "A Reason to Hope : A Synthesis of **Teilhard de Chardin's** Vision and Systems Thinking", **R. Wayne Kraft** writes:

> **"The unique feature of Teilhard's vision is that it is a Christian interpretation of evolution. His vision is based upon, and was greatly influenced by, the work of Charles Darwin. But Teilhard goes far beyond Darwin. Teilhard's thought encompasses the whole cosmos, not merely the development of life on earth.**
>
> **Teilhard's contribution to mankind is that he has shown us how to reconcile the extremes exemplified by the creationists and the evolutionists. Both the religious fundamentalists and the scientific fundamentalists err when they think they have a monopoly on the truth of creation. Teilhard has shown how creation is a divine process. Creation by evolution is what occurs." [110]**

Order and direction are basic characteristics of our dynamic universe. It is hard to believe that order in the constantly changing universe is a product of mere arbitrariness, that billions of processes cohere by accident at every moment. Without coherence, an advance in the general direction to life is unthinkable, demanding as it does increasingly orderly arrangements. It is easy to see the guiding hand of God in the realization of this. The interplay between necessity and chance allows "plenty of room" for His movements.

Theology understands God to be both transcendent and immanent. He is not merely a cosmic "watch maker" who once

Chapter 3 — Evolving Universe

wound up the watch - e.g. created the universe and then made an exit. God creates, sustains, cares about the world all the time. **Arthur Peacocke** said :

> "It is the realization....... that the cosmos which is sustained and held in being by God is a cosmos which has always been in process of producing new emergent forms of matter - it is a creatio continua, as it has long been called in Christian theology. God creates continuously - 'all the time', as we would say." [111]

John Polkinghorne, a physicist and theologian, wrote:

> "Providence is closely assimilated to creation. Indeed it becomes the everyday experience of the creative process in a world which is sustained in being by its Creator. Ian Barbour says of such ideas that it would be desirable to merge the traditional doctrines of creation and providence into a doctrine of *continuing creation*." [112, 113]

The understanding of God Who is transcendent and immanent is called *panentheism*, defined

> "as the belief that the Being of God includes and penetrates the whole universe, so that every part of it exists in Him, but that His Being is more than, and is not exhausted by, the universe." [114]

The term *contingency* had already been used in pre-Christian philosophy to express the opposite of necessity. The idea of contingency from the Christian viewpoint was elaborated by **Thomas Torrance.**

Thomas Torrance is Professor Emeritus at the University of Edinburgh in the UK and former moderator of the General Assembly of the Church of Scotland. He holds doctorates in theology, philosophy of science and literature. He is editor of the book series entitled "Theology and Science at the Frontiers of Knowledge." He holds honorary degrees from several universities, and is Protopresbyter of the Greek Orthodox Church.

His writings about contingency include the teachings of Basil (the Great) of Caesarea, John Chrysostom and Gregory of Nazianzus, the so-called "Three Hierarchs" of the fourth century.

SCIENCE AND FAITH

> "Contingent things do not have to be and contingent events do not have to happen. They can be and not be, but once they are, they are what they are in dependence on something else which is not itself contingent.
>
> ... The universe is understood to have come into existence out of nothing freely through the will and power of God, as something utterly distinct from God and utterly dependent upon his ordering interaction with it. While the universe might have been other than it is, it came into being not without divine reason. Far from being merely an arbitrary product of God's will, the creation is regarded as having had its origin in the love of God....." [115]

With a fondness for the Three Hierarchs and a deep knowledge of physics, Torrance also writes:

> "Under God we have been rediscovering the contingent nature of the universe and its open-textured order which point beyond themselves altogether to the transcendent source and ground of their rationality in the Word of God. That is the very Word who become flesh in Jesus Christ, our Lord and Saviour." [116]

There is no intrinsic necessity for the universe to exist and to progress. However, it exists and it progresses. We often take for granted the processes met along the path of the general direction to life. But thinking deeply about them, we may wish to say a prayer with humility: thank you, God, for the miracle of our existence, for the possibility of spiritual development and hope for eternal life in love.

I remember a letter which I received in my youth from a friend who later become a priest. He wrote:

> "I walked on a bridge across the Danube in Budapest. The mighty river flowed beneath me. I watched it and was filled with wonder. It is a miracle, I thought, that the world exists, that I am here on this bridge and I can in my insufficient way, absorb the beauty of nature."

Chapter 3 — Evolving Universe

Human Beings as God's Collaborators

Do we have value in our universe?

Paul Davies, professor of theoretical physics, stresses consciousness as an exceptional human quality :

> "We who are children of the universe - animated stardust - can nevertheless reflect on the nature of that same universe, even to the extent of glimpsing the rules on which it runs.
>
> What is Man that we might be party to such privilege? I cannot believe that our existence in this universe is a mere quirk of fate, an accident of history, an incidental blip in the great cosmic drama. Our involvement is too intimate. The physical species Homo may count for nothing, but the existence of mind in some organism on some planet in the universe is surely a fact of fundamental significance. Through conscious beings the universe has generated self-awareness. This can be no trivial detail, no minor by-product of mindless, purposeless forces. We are truly meant to be here." [117]
>
> "The knowledge that our presence in the universe represents a fundamental rather than an incidental feature of existence offers, I believe, a deep and satisfying basis for human dignity." [118]

The spiritual component of a human being, rather than the physical one, distinguishes him or her from other living beings.

Sam Berry, biologist, Professor of Genetics, University of London, President European Ecological Federation, Member, General Synod of the Church of England:

> "We are distinguished from the rest of creation by God's image in us (Gen 1:26-27), not genetically or anatomically. ... the important element is that we are subject and responsible to God in a qualitatively different way to the rest of creation." [119]

The general direction to life does not stop at human existence.

SCIENCE AND FAITH

Human beings may take part in the evolutionary process which now embraces spirituality. Human beings have a wonderful opportunity to be God's collaborators, but they can use this opportunity only if love directs their actions. They can approach God only through love.

We can take no credit for the evolutionary journey from hot, dense plasma to life; we can almost say that it was presented to us. From one point of view we are entitled to think that we are extremely valuable; understanding that the universe is not purposeless, that general direction to life exists and that we have the opportunity to be God's collaborators gives our life meaning as well as great responsibility. From another point of view, understanding that we have done nothing to deserve the cosmic evolution should make us very humble and thankful to God.

We have free will. Human history describes the evolution of societies, including wars and struggles for power, but also tells a story of compassion. It is true that human beings may follow the general direction to death rather than to life. They may kill and have hate in their hearts;they may be cold and egotistic, totally indifferent to the needs of their neighbours in whatever society they live. But there is also a gamut of positive qualities: contemplation (in Russian *sozertsanie*) of God, intuitive understanding of what is good and bad, goodness, intelligence, scientific thought which seeks to comprehend nature. Those who have contributed to the spiritual evolution have been sources of light to illumine history's path.

God did not create ideal beings but He gave us the possibility to be good and we are responsible for the realization of our own potential. God helps us all, but our own effort is vital.

John Polkinghorne wrote:

> **"The one who is love " (God) " will grant a generous measure of independence to his world, for love is grounded in the free interchange between lover and beloved. The God of love can be no cosmic puppet master, pulling the strings of a world which is totally subservient to him." [120]**

The key word is again achievement. If we did not have free will we should have neither personal achievements nor any

Chapter 3 — Evolving Universe

individuality. In the world of opposite directions, human beings have the opportunity to choose love. Whichever direction they choose, they will meet resistance. The balance between good and evil can shift to the side of good which is why we pray for love in our lives and for eternal life in love.

> "He said therefore, 'What is the kingdom of God like? And to what shall I compare it? It is like a grain of mustard seed which a man took and sowed in his garden;and it grew and became a tree, and the birds of the air made nests in its branches.'"
> (Luke 13 / 18, 19) [2]

> "Thy kingdom come.
> Thy will be done,
> On earth as it is in heaven."
> (Matthew 6 / 10) [2] "Our Father"

In to-day's diverse world I wish it were possible to see: more people accepting belief in God who is love, and more understanding between different religions; more compassion in the world. I wish that the feeling we are all God's children could replace the "holy" feeling of belonging to a race, a nation or an ideology, and that we could develop global thinking, global ethics. I should like to see the development of individual responsibility which is impossible under dictatorship of any kind. I should like to see more concern for the environment.

In spite of all the evil in the world, I do believe in the power of love.

Time

The Babylonians, ancient Greeks, Romans, the Eastern religions, the Chinese, the Mayas and Norse mythology, spoke of cyclical time. [121, 122] Time is related to events. "Good" times when people are happy, and "bad" times replace each other; up and down, up and down, time rotates as a wheel. If this is so, "before" and "after" have little sense. Such a universe could last for ever. Still, if each cycle could contribute in some way to the next one, such a universe might relate to the idea of progress.

SCIENCE AND FAITH

Among the religions of the ancient world, Judaism was different in its concept of time. Judaism and Christianity accept linear time and the concept that events are unique, non-repetitive. God created the world and time as well. **St Augustine** said :

> **"Let them understand that before all time began you (God) are the eternal Creator of all time, and that no time and no created thing is co-eternal with you...."** [123]

St. Augustine asserted that God made the world

"with time and not in time". [124]

Time's linearity is related to the development of the universe; and this concept does not exclude awareness of periodical changes which are part of our life, changes of seasons or changes between day and night, for these are related to the Earth's rotation. We know that spring will follow winter. There is a stability in the repetition of phenomena and we rely on it. Periodical changes have helped develop time measurements and the time unit.* However, this year's spring is not the same as last year's.

Everything is different. Together with some repetition in forms, there is irreversibility. We and the world are one year older.

Classical physics assumes that time is absolute, and that determinism makes predictions of the future theoretically possible. Neither of these assumptions have survived in to-day's scientific view.

The theory of relativity objects to the existence of absolute time, for time does not "flow" at an even rate. According to the Special theory of relativity, the time of an event, measured by two observers, depends on their position and motion, and there is no way of deciding which time is correct. "Now" is related to "here". Time will be "shorter" or "longer" depending on the velocity of the observer. However, time dilation effects are significant only if the velocities of motion are close to the speed of light. But no observer will see that consequences occur before cause. The principle of

---

* The relatively new definition of a second, the time unit, is based on the radiation of the isotope of Cesium Cs^{133}; this definition is given in comparison with the former one based on the Earth's rotation around the sun.

Chapter 3 — Evolving Universe

causality is not abolished.

As mentioned in discussing the theory of relativity, theoretical predictions are experimentally verified.

Time also depends on gravity, according to the General theory of relativity. These effects are also verified by experiment. Time intervals measured at the bottom of a mountain are a little longer than those measured by the same device at the top of the mountain. Although the differences are small, they are measurable. For an observer approaching a black hole (!), time would pass very slowly.

According to the theory of relativity, space and time are related and cannot be considered separately. The configuration of a four-dimensional entity space-time depends on the distribution of mass and energy. In a mutual interconnection, time and space, as part of the holistic picture, are affected by everything which happens in the universe and vice versa. Space and time were created with the Big Bang; a question about space and time outside the universe is meaningless. The dynamic, expanding universe seems to have had a beginning at a finite time in the past, and at a finite time in the future the whole universe will either recollapse into a state of infinite density, or will be in a state of complete disorder.

There is an opinion that the theory of relativity to-day gives the most complete description of time. However, the theory of relativity leaves open the question of why there should be "arrows of time".

Arthur Eddington, astrophysicist, used this notion of the *arrow of time* which is related to time's asymmetrical processes, to irreversibility.

The second law of thermodynamics describes time's asymmetrical processes. The law can be expressed in different ways; as mentioned, its meaning is often given in the statement that "the entropy of an isolated system can never decrease". The notion of an "isolated system" is really an idealization; there is some uncertainty in applying the inevitable increase of entropy to the whole cosmos. Still, we understand that the increase of entropy has more than a local character;it is a cosmic phenomenon, and by relating it to the time arrow, we imply that the time arrow exists for the universe, not merely for local events. The increase of entropy happens in time, thus making it possible to distinguish between past and future; there will be more entropy in the future than there was in the past. It is almost impossible to discuss the very difficult question of time without touching the second law of thermodynamics.

The laws of physics are generally symmetrical in time. Equations of the laws of mechanics, electromagnetism, nuclear physics etc. are independent of time. Do natural phenomena exist which are asymmetrical in time and irreversible like the second law of thermodynamics?

Well, there are some. Expansion of the universe has been discussed as a time asymmetrical process. Perhaps, however, the universe will contract instead of continue to expand. To-day's opinion is that if contraction replaces expansion, entropy will still increase, so time will not go backwards.

There are other asymmetrical processes which could be related to the time arrow: the aging process of living beings; the psychological time arrow (we remember what happened in the past but do not know the future);the decay of neutral K - meson (some irreversibility here seems insignificant); the emission of electromagnetic radiation (cannot be emitted from a source into the past, only into the future). [121, 122]

Still, in most discussions, the arrow of time is related to the increase of entropy.

Could the processes along the general direction to life also be used to express the time arrow? It seems yes. The processes of cosmic evolution, the most important processes in the universe, even in our qualitative understanding of them, also describe the time arrow. These processes are not less real than the spontaneous increase of entropy. Prigogine talks about the progressive rediscovery of time. The time in which the whole cosmic evolution occurs, the time of increasing orderly complexity in the world, seem completely different to that time relating to the second law of thermodynamics.

Perhaps both descriptions of the time arrow are related to the same reality. Talking of the dissipative structures which may appear in an open system, far from equilibrium, Prigogine stresses that they need a constant supply of energy and export of entropy into the surroundings; without exporting entropy they could not exist. Formation of any orderly structures, under any circumstances, generally occurs only with an increase in total entropy.

Take Fig. 2 : both the general direction to life and the general direction to death advance simultaneously towards opposite goals. Both are irreversible (so each can be related to the time arrow) and

Chapter 3 — Evolving Universe

both are interconnected.

At least the advance to life does not occur without the advance to death, although it would be incorrect to say vice versa. Both general directions, each a possible description of the time arrow, are opposite and united. We live in a universe in which achievements and approach to the end occur simultaneously.

To-day's science predicts that at one step of the cosmic evolution life in any form will cease to exist. Then there will be nobody to be aware of the universe and time. The universe will be purposeless, its potentials almost exhausted. If this happens, time will perhaps be associated only with the general direction to death. What meaning could time have at all in a dark, almost empty universe, or a universe contracted into a singularity? It seems that when both general directions reach their ends, the question of time will no longer have any meaning. Does time play any role in a spiritual, eternal life in love ?

SCIENCE AND FAITH

CONCLUSION

Science Motivates My Belief in God

We have discussed the basic characteristics of nature, its order and rationality. Without these orderly arrangements there would be, in all probability, no world at all, no life and no science. The order does not maintain a static world, but a dynamic one in which, along with processes of degeneration, we see an evolution towards orderly complexity, towards life, towards spirituality.

Many scientists have become aware of this through their work, and we have seen that they have used expressions such as:

> "**Divine order of the world's structure...
> wonderful arrangement and harmony of the
> cosmos...
> the order, the symmetry, the harmony...
> harmony which maintains the order of the
> universe...
> purposefulness...
> overwhelming evidence of an intelligence and
> benevolent intention...
> the magnitude, the beauty and the harmony of
> His creation...
> the harmony of natural law which reveals an
> intelligence of such superiority that...
> the universe...looks more like a great thought
> than like a great machine...
> the divine order of the world's structure..."**

An awareness of this coherence in nature leads to awareness of God, the creator and sustainer of the universe. Scientists talk of :

> "**The builder who creates all...
> the plan of an almighty and omniscient being...**

SCIENCE AND FAITH

He is the originator of the universal harmony...
the eternal existence of creative and almighty wisdom...
superior intelligence...
the clearest proof of a creative intelligence, of its providence, wisdom and power...
the greatness and infinite wisdom of the Creator...
eternal creator-ruler...
no doubt of the reality of His (God's) existence...
the discovery of natural law is a meeting with God...
human beings understand the law, but did not create it...
a superior mind that reveals itself in the world of experience...
the profoundest reason and the most radiant beauty...
central order..."

Physicist **Max Planck** expressed the idea that science brings an acceptance of God's existence like this:

"For the believers God is in the beginning and for physicists He is at the end of all considerations". [50]

With many others, **Arthur Peacocke,** molecular biologist and theologian, also approached God through science :

"In my youth I became an agnostic. But I was terribly impressed, as I did research, that the universe really was intelligible. Why does nature always turn out to be more intellectually coherent than anything we can conceive before we do the studies? I believe the universe is rational because there is a suprarational Being behind it.

I am thrilled by the beauty and rationality of the Universe, from quarks to the human brain, its order, intricacy and integration.

I believe God is the ultimate reality. God is eternal, beyond space and time." [125]

Chapter — Conclusion

The wonderful *order* in nature is an undeniable fact. We investigate a rational, coherent world. No wonder then, that this investigation leads to God. It is difficult if not impossible to accept the idea that such order occurred only by mere chance.

The second undeniable fact is *cosmic evolution*. The evolution of life is only a part of the cosmic evolution.

> **"Cosmic evolution means universal change. It applies to all aspects of evolution : particulate, galactic, stellar, elemental, chemical, biological, cultural. All are part of it."** – Eric Chaisson, astrophysicist. [75]

Order in nature makes it possible for the world to exist and to evolve through many steps from quarks to the human brain, even more importantly, to a feeling of love which is God's spark in us. A realization of the potentials of the universe occurs in evolution without the iron rule of determinism; it proceeds in an interplay of chance and necessity. Human existence and the possibility for our spiritual development does not seem to have been haphazard, rather the result of an act by the caring hand of God. We quoted physicist Robert Boyd: "I see the whole process from beginning to end" (from Big Bang to the occurrence of *homo religiensis*) "as the Act of God".

The opportunity is given to us to be God's collaborators on the path of the general direction to life. The certain existence of this direction also speaks about the purpose of the universe, about God and the meaning of our life.

The physical death of individuals is inevitable and the extinction of life in any form is most probable in the distant future. The potential of the universe is realized in progress but is increasingly lost. Is death really the end of all those achievements at so many levels of the cosmic evolution? I do not believe so. I deeply believe in an eternal spiritual life in love, and in the invitation we have received to step into this life. Why do I mix ethics, spirituality and love with physics and other natural sciences? The point of this book is to approach religion through science. It is true that ethics, spirituality and love belong to a category of our perceptions apart

SCIENCE AND FAITH

from physics, astronomy, chemistry, or biology. However, the whole path of the general direction to life is unique and includes spirituality and love. In observing natural processes we learn that later levels of cosmic evolution give meaning to prior ones.

The awareness of order and harmony in the world is as old as science. In the last several decades particularly, with the development of cosmology, the idea of cosmic evolution has become widely accepted as a part of our view of the world. **Robert Jastrow**, astrophysicist, said half jokingly :

> **"He (the scientist) has scaled the mountains of ignorance; he is about to conquer the highest peak; as he pulls himself over the final rock, he is greeted by a band of theologians who have been sitting there for centuries."[126]**

Theologians and scientists have not now met each other for the first time; those who were broad-minded, not exclusive, were always on the same path.

In all the many different approaches to religion there is: a feeling of love; an intuitive comprehension of God's presence in the world and in our life; an understanding that ethical ideas of good and bad are more deeply rooted in us than the standards prescribed by the society in which we live. *One of the approaches to religion, to God, is through science. One of my reasons for believing in God is my scientific understanding of a nature with meaning.* Although for me this approach is very logical and very convincing, I cannot say that science proves God's existence. With many others I can, however, say that *science motivates my belief in God.*

From my Russian colleagues I heard an anecdote about the famous physiology professor **Ivan Pavlov**. After the 1918 revolution, propaganda tried to convince people that religion was a comfort of the uneducated. After a service in one of Leningrad's (now St. Petersburg's) churches, a modestly-dressed man came out and sat on a bench in front of the church. A militiaman, himself uneducated, saw the older man, approached him and said ironically: "What, old man, you prayed in the church?" The man answered "Yes, I did". "Silly, ignorant old man", mocked the militiaman rudely. Later, to his surprise, the militiaman discovered that the old man was the

Chapter — Conclusion

respected and famous Pavlov.

Cleverness, intelligence, decency and honesty are not, of course, qualities to be found only in educated people. I wish only to say it is wrong to think that a scientific education makes us disbelievers in God; just the opposite is true. I also wish to say we must love everybody, including the militiaman.

Love

Love is the source of all virtues and of the greatest happiness; love is forever; God is love.

> "So we know and believe the love God has for us. GOD IS LOVE, and he who abides in love abides in God, and God abides in him." (1 John 4/16) [2]

> "Love never ends;" (1 Corinthians 13/8) [2]

The theologian Nikolai Arseniev embraces St. Augustine's thought:

> "Augustine was right when instead of formulating external rules of moral conduct he made this bold enunciation : "Dilige et fac quod vis" ("Love, and do what you like"). He was really stating hereby the inner sense of the whole moral teaching of the Gospel.
>
> But it is more than a moral teaching; it is a new force - the stream of divine love connecting heaven and earth and giving a sense, a direction to our lives still here on earth." [127]

The goal of the general direction to life is not only something which is coming, it is also partly here, now. There is something wrong if we fight in the name of love, thus annihilating the meaning of the word.

Early in my career at the University of Belgrade, I was sometimes visited by an elderly engineer. Every two or three months he brought me his writings about atomic structures. His son also visited me, explaining how important those notes were to his father, almost a "raison d'être" in his retirement. He had the feeling that he was doing something which could perhaps be useful to students. He

SCIENCE AND FAITH

always came with a worried look, as if he were not sure how I would receive his papers. I tried to be kind and always said that I looked at them and found them interesting. And this was true. I had the impression that when he left, he was happier then when he arrived.

I once started to talk to him about religion. My colleagues at the faculty knew that I was a believer and that I went to church. It was inadvisable, in those days, for a university professor to do this, but they tolerated me. There was no question of my discussing religion in front of a group of students;I dared do this only when alone with an individual. What a coward I was!

Well, as I said, the conversation between the elderly engineer and myself turned to God. This was unavoidable;then as now I thought that science led to God. To my unpleasant surprise, the engineer expressed his atheistic views, and our arguments escalated. I became annoyed, irritated and rude. There was bitterness in us both when we said goodbye, and what I noticed too late, being in such a bad mood, he was unhappy. He needed me.

For three months, four, five and six, my engineer never came. Perhaps he thought that I should be unkind, on account of our differences about religion. He died after six months had passed, and less than a year after that his son died in a car accident.

Probably the engineer's death had nothing to do with our discussion during his last visit. Probably his son's accident had nothing to do with his father's death. Perhaps I was not so guilty as I later thought. I have certainly done worse things in my life. Still, I was very unkind in the name of religion; in the name of God who is love I did not show love. Could I not have expressed my opinion in a kind way?

People are capable of killing in the name of "holy" ideas, without understanding that love is the epitome of holiness. How wrong it is to think that the end justifies the means.

> **"Love is patient and kind; love is not jealous or boastful; it is not arrogant or rude. Love does not insist on its own way;it is not irritable or resentful;it does not rejoice at wrong, but rejoices in the right."**
> **(1 Corinthians 13/4-6) [2]**

Chapter — Conclusion

Love as an idea only, as a principle, without including patience and kindness, is simply not love. Love is a divine seed which can blossom in us. Love is everyday care for others, a warm feeling for anybody in the world who suffers.

We can be at no time happier than when love permeates our feelings, our thoughts and activities. I know there is something wrong with me if I am not happier upon leaving the church after the liturgy than I was upon entering; it means that I have failed to open my heart and receive the divine love offered to me. Love is joy.

Love is an enormous power which slowly conquers. Eternal life in love is the goal of the general direction to life and our individual goal as well. The theologian **Kallistos Ware** wrote:

> **"To say to another, with all our heart, 'I love you', is to say, 'You will never die.'"** [128]

Finally, I would like to quote from the famous mathematician **Leonhard Euler (1707-1783)**.

There are Euler's differential equations, Euler's function, Euler's number etc. He was extremely productive, even during the last decade of his life when he was blind. Thanks to his memory and his capacity for concentration he could dictate mathematical ideas and derivations to his students. At that period, he "wrote" among other things, a book on optics in which, despite his blindness, he discussed the theory of astronomic telescopes.

He asked:

> **"How will it be in the other life where the Almighty Himself will fill us with his love? With a love whose blessed effects will be uninterrupted by change. This must be a happiness beyond anything which we can imagine in our present state."** [129]

SCIENCE AND FAITH

REFERENCES

1. "Good News Bible", American Bible Society, New York, 1976.
2. "The New Oxford Annotated Bible with the Apocrypha", Revised standard version, Oxford University Press, 1977.
3. Alexander Semyonov, "The God Who Couldn't Be Hidden", in "Scientists Who Believe", ed. Eric Barret and David Fischer, Moody Press, Chicago, 1984, p.98.
4. Blaise Pascal, "Pensées", [282], The Modern Library, New York, 1941, p.96.
5. John Polkinghorne, "God's Action in the World", CTNS (The Center for Theology and the Natural Sciences) Bulletin, Vol.10, No. 2, Spring 1990.
6. Richard Bube, "The Failure of the God-of-the-Gaps", in "Horizons of Science", ed. Carl Henry, Harper and Row, New York, 1978, p. 26.
7. "The Complete Poetical Works of Percy Bysshe Shelley", Humphrey Milford, Oxford University Press, Oxford, reprinted 1943, Adonais LII, p. 438.
8. Walter Heitler, "Stufen der Belebung und der unverwesliche Leib", in "Die Befreiung vom wissenschaftlichen Glaube", ed. Heinrich Zoller, Herderbucherei, Freiburg im Breisgau, Band 489, p.133.
9. Friedrich Dessauer, "Religion im Lichte der Heutigen Naturwissenschaft", Verlag Josef Knecht, Frankfurt am Main, 1956, p. 44.
10. "Ideas and Opinions by Albert Einstein", ed. Carl Seelig, Bonanza Books, New York, 1954, p. 262.
11. Eugene Mallove, "The Quickening Universe", St. Martin's Press, New York, 1987, p. 228.
12. Ref. 10, p. 40.
13. "Quantum Questions", ed.Ken Wilber, New Science Library, Boston and London, 1985, p. 17.
14. Ernst Frankenberger, "Gottbekenntnisse grosser Naturforscher", Johannes Verlag, Leutesdorf am Rhein, 6.Auflage 1973, p. 7.
15. Ref.14, p. 7.
16. Edgar Hunger, "Von Demokrit bis Heisenberg", Friedr. Vieweg und Sohn, Braunschweig, 1964, 4. Auflage, Erster Teil, p. 52.
17. Ref.13, p. 61.
18. Werner Heisenberg, "Across the Frontiers", Harper and Row, New York, 1974, p. 215.
19. Walter Heitler, "Die Natur und das Gottliche", Verlag Kett und Balmer, Zug, 2. Auflage, 1975, p. 129.
20. Ref. 14, p. 8.
21. Ref. 14, p. 9.

SCIENCE AND FAITH

22. Milan Marković, "Religija nauke", in the journal "Pravoslavlje" (Orthodoxy), Beograd, May 1976.
23. Ref.14, p.9.
24. Ref.14, p.9.
25. Ref.14, p.10.
26. Ref.14, p.10.
27. Ref.14, p.10.
28. Ref.14, p.11.
29. Ref.14, p.11.
30. Phillip Eichman, "Michael Faraday : Man of God - Man of Science", Perspective on Science and Christian Faith, Vol.40, No.2, 1988, pp.91-97.
31. Ref.30, Quotation : J.F.Riley, "The Hammer and the Anvil", The Dalkesman Publ.Co., 1954, pp.2, 3.
32. Ref.14, p.12.
33. Ref.14, p.12.
34. Ref.14, p.13.
35. Ref.14, p.14.
36. Ref.14, p.14
37. Ref.14, p.15.
38. Ref.14.p.19.
39. Franz Stuhlhofer, "Naturforscher und die Frage nach Gott", Schwengeler Verlag, Berneck, 1988, p.47.
40. "Chto govoryat o Boge sovremennie ucheniye", ed.R.Kurtua, Imprimerie A.Rosseels, Louvain, Belgique, 1960, p.34, 35.
41. Ref.14, p.20.
42. Ref.40, p.44.
43. Ref.14, p.19.
44. Ref.14, p.26.
45. Ref.14, p.17.
46. Hubert Muschalek, "Gottbekenntnisse moderner Naturforscher", Morus Verlag, Berlin, 4.Auflage 1964, p.219.
47. Ref. 40, p. 11.
48. Ref.46, pp.53, 54. John Templeton, "The Humble Approach", The Seabury Press, New York, 1981, p.15. "Physik und Transzendenz", ed.Hans-Peter Dürr, Scherz Verlag, Bern, 1988, p.64.
49. Ref.46, p.86.
50. Max Planck, "Religion und Naturwissenschaft", Johannes Ambrosius Barth Verlag, Leipzig, 1958. Ref.46, pp.80-84. Ref.16, Zweiter Teil pp.58-60.
51. Werner Heisenberg, "Physics and Beyond", Harper Torchbooks, New York 1971, pp.214-216.
52. "Physik und Transzendenz", ed. Hans-Peter Dürr, Scherz Verlag, Bern, 1988, p.227.

References

53. Ref.19, pp.129, 130.
54. Erwin Schrödinger, "What is Life?" and "Mind and Matter", Cambridge University Press, Cambridge, 1977, p.165.
55. Ref.51, pp.209, 210.
56. Enrico Cantore, "Scientific Man", ISH (Institute of Scientific Humanism) Publication, New York, 1977, p.104, from A.Einstein "Prologue to Max Planck : Where is Science going?", trans.J.Murphy, Norton, 1932, p.11.
57. Ref.56, p.440. Statement reported by H.Reichenbach in "Albert Einstein, Philosopher - Scientist", ed. P.A.Schlipp, Harper Torchbooks, 1959, p.292.
58. Ref.10, p.11.
59. Ref.14, p.25.
60. Michael Pupin, "From Immigrant to Inventor", Charls Scribner's Sons, New York, 1930, p.282.
61. Ref.14, p.21.
62. Ref.40, p.22.
63. Ref.46, p.269.
64. Enrico Cantore, "Science as an Experience of the Absolute : Religious and Moral Implications of Research".Proceedings of the Sixth International Conference of the Unity of the Sciences, San Francisco, 1977, reprinted from "The Search for Absolute Values in a Changing World", 1978, The International Cultural Foundation, Inc. p.1153.
65. Jack Lousma, "Twenty-four Million Mile Man", in "Scientists Who Believe," eds.Eric Barret and David Fischer, Moody Press, Chicago, 1984 (Ref.3), p.114.
66. Frederick Trinklein, "The God of Science", William Eerdmans Publ.Comp., Grand Rapids, Michigan, 1971, p.62.
67. Ian Barbour, "Ways of Relating Science and Theology", in "Physics, Philosophy and Theology", eds.Robert Russel, William Stoeger and Georghe Coyne, Vatican Observatory - Vatican City State, University of Notre Dame Press, Notre Dame, 1988, p.34.
68. Ref.11, p.xiii.
69. Ref.11, p.230.
70. John Gribbin and Martin Rees, "Cosmic Coincidences", Bantam Books, New York, 1989, pp.3, 4.
71. John Barrow, "The World within the World", Oxford University Press, Oxford, 1990, p.228.
72. Jonathan Halliwell, "Quantum Cosmology and the Creation of the Universe", Scientific American, December 1991, p.26.
73. John Barrow, "Theories of Everything", Clarendon Press, Oxford, 1991, p.167.
74. Joseph Silk, "The Big Bang", W. H. Freeman and Comp., San Francisco, 1980, p.63.
75. Erich Chaisson, "Cosmic Evolution; The Religion of a Scientist", IRAS (Institute on Religion in an Age of Science) Newsletter, Oct.1991, Vol.40, No.1.
76. Henri Bergson, "Creative Evolution", MacMillan, London, 1964.

SCIENCE AND FAITH

77. Teilhard de Chardin, "The Phenomenon of Man", Harper and Row, New York, 1959. Teilhard de Chardin, "Hymn of the Universe", William Collins Sons, London, and Harper and Row, New York, 1981. R.Wayne Kraft, "A Reason to Hope : A Synthesis of Teilhard de Chardin's Vision and Systems Thinking", Intersystem, Seaside, 1983.

78. Walter Heitler, "Der Mensch und die Naturwissenschaftliche Erkenntnis", Friedrich Vieweg und Sohn, Braunschweig, 4.Auflage, 1970. Walter Heitler, "Naturphilosophische Streifzuge", Friedrich Vieweg und Sohn, Braunschweig, 1970. Walter Heitler, ""Die Natur und das Gottliche", Verlag Klett und Balmer, Zug, 2.Auflage 1975. Walter Heitler, "Stufen der Belebung und der unverwesliche Leib", in "Die Befreiung vom wissenschaftlichen Glauben", ed.Heinrich Zoller, Herderbücherei, Band 489, Freiburg im Breisgau 1974.

79. Holmes Rolston III, "Science and Religion", Random House, New York, 1987.

80. Paul Davies, "The Cosmic Blueprint", Simon and Schuster, New York 1988. Paul Davies, "The Mind of God", Simon and Schuster, New York, 1992.

81. Ref.80. Paul Davies, "The Cosmic Blueprint", Simon and Schuster, New York, 1988, p.20.

82. John Borrow and Frank Tipler, "The Anthropic Cosmological Principle", Oxford University Press, Oxford, 1988, p.1. Quotation Brandon Carter in "Confrontation of Cosmological Theories with Observation", ed. M.S.Longair, Reidel, Dordrecht, 1974, p.291.

83. Ref.82, p.21.

84. Ref.79, pp.69 and 79, Quotation B.J.Carr and M.J.Rees, "The Anthropic Principle and the Structure of the Physical World", Nature 278, 1979, pp.605, 609.

85. Ref.79, pp.69 and 79, Quotation Bernard Lovell, "Whence?", New York Times Magazine, November 16, 1975, pp.85, 89.

86. Paul Davies, "The Accidental Universe", Cambridge University Press, Cambridge, 1982, p.118.

87. Ref.79, pp.69 and 80, Quotation Freeman J.Dyson, "Energy in the Universe", Scientific American, 225, 1971, p.59.

88. Ref.79, pp.70 and 80, Quotation Mike Corwin, "From Chaos to Consciousness", Astronomy 11, 1983, pp.16, 17, 19.

89. Ref.79, pp.70 and 80, Quotation George Wald, "Fitness in the Universe : Choices and Necessities", in J.Oró et.al., eds., "Cosmochemical Evolution and the Origins of Life", Dodrecht, , D.Reidel Publ.Co., 1974, pp.8, 9.

90. Ref.79, pp.69 and 79, Quotation Dietrick E.Thomsen, "In the Beginning Was Quantum Gravity", Science News 124, No.10, pp.152, 153, 157.

91. Ilya Prigogine, "From Being to Becoming", W.H. Freeman and Co., New York, 1980.

92. Ilya Prigogine and Isabelle Stengers, "Order out of Chaos", New Science Library, Boulder and London, 1984.

93. Ref.71, pp.271-274.

94. Ref.73, pp.123, 124.

95. J.T.Houghton, "New Ideas of Chaos in Physics", Science and Christian Belief, 1, 1989, pp.41-51.

References

96. Ref.91, p. XII.
97. Ref.91, p.XIII.
98. D.J.Bartholomew, "Probability, Belief and Truth", in"Can Scientists Believe", ed.Sir Nevill Mott, James and James, London, 1991, p.54.
99. Arthur Peacocke, "Intimations of Reality", University of Notre Dame Press, Notre Dame, 1984, pp.70-72.
100. T.V.Smith, "Philosophers Speak for Themselves", The University of Chicago Press, 1942.
101. Ref.19, p.58.
102. Andrew Miller, "Biology and Belief", in "Real Science, Real Faith", ed. R.J.Berry, Monarch, Eastbourne, 1991, pp.77-79.
103. Ref.102, pp. 89 and 95
104. R.P.Wayne," Atmospheric Chemistry: The Evolution of our Atmosphere", Journal of Photochemistry and Photobiology, A:Chem., 62, 1992, 379-396.
105. Ref.48, John Templeton, "The Humble Approach", The Seabury Press, New York, 1981, p.92.
106. Ref.79, pp.72 and 80, Quotation Victor Weisskopf, "The Origin of the Universe", American Scientists 71, 1983, p.480.
107. Alan Hayward, "God is. A scientist shows why it makes sense to believe in God", Thomas Nelson Publ., Nashville, 1980, p.196.
108. Semiramis Dionysiou-Kouimtzi, "Science in My Christian Belief", in "Can Scientists Believe", ed. Sir Nevill Mott, James and James, London, 1991, pp.161, 162.
109. R.L.F.Boyd, "The Space Sciences", in "Horizons of Science", ed.Carl F.H.Henry, Harper and Row, New York, 1978, p.15.
110. Ref.77, R.Wayne Kraft, "A Reason to Hope : A Synthesis of Teilhard de Chardin's Vision and Systems Thinking", Intersystems Publ., Seaside, 1983, p.20.
111. Ref.99, pp.62, 63.
112. John Polkinghorne, "Science and Providence", New Science Library, Boston, 1989, pp.40, 41.
113. Ian Barbour, "Issues in Science and Religion", Harper Torchbooks, New York, 1966, p.417.
114. Ref.99, pp.64 and 89, according to "Oxford Dictionary of the Christian Church", 1.edition, ed.F.L.Cross, Oxford University Press, 1970, p.1010.
115. Thomas Torrance, "Divine and Contingent Order", Oxford University Press, 1981, pp.85 and 10.
116. Thomas Torrance, "The Christian Frame of Mind", Helmers and Howard, Colorado Springs, 1989, p.15.
117. Ref.80. Paul Davies, "The Mind of God", Simon and Schuster, New York, 1992, p.232.
118. Ref.81, p.203.
119. Sam Berry, "Genes, Genesis and Greens", in "Real Science, Real Faith", ed.R.J.Berry, Monarch, Eastbourne, 1991, p.186.

SCIENCE AND FAITH

120. John Polkinghorne, "Science and Creation", New Science Library, Boston, 1989, p.52.
121. Richard Morris, "Time's Arrows", A Touchstone Book, Simon and Schuster, New York, 1985.
122. "Zeit im Wandel der Zeit", ed. Peter Aichelburg, Vieweg and Sohn, Braunschweig/Wiesbaden, 1988.
123. Ref.99, pp.62 and 89, Quotation St.Augustine "Confessions", ch.11, paras. 14, 30, trans.R.S.Pinecoffin, Harmondsworth, Penguin Classics, 1961, 263, 279.
124. Ref.117, p.42.
125. Arthur Peacocke, "Who is God", Magazine "Life", Dec.1990, pp.47-78.
126. Robert Jastrow, "God and the Astronmomers", Warner Books, New York, 1978, pp.105, 106.
127. Nicholas Arseniev, "Revelation of Life Eternal", St.Vladimir's Seminary Press, Crestwood, New York, 1982, p.143.
128. Kallistos Ware, "The Orthodox Way", in USA published by St.Vladimir's Orthodox Theological Seminary, Crestwood, New York, 1979, p.26 (in Great Britain published by Hunt Barnard Printing).
129. Ref. 39, p.61.

SELECT BIBLIOGRAPHY

Adams Richard Newbold, "The Eighth Day" (Social Evolution as the Self-Organization of Energy), Univ.of Texas Press, Austin, 1988.

Aichelburg Peter, ed., "Zeit im Wandel der Zeit", Vieweg, Braunschweig, 1988. (Eichelburg, Aristoteles, Plotin, Augustinus, Kant, Mach, Boltzmann, Poincaré, Bergson, Russel, Minkowski, Reichenbach, Wiener, Piaget, Goedel, von Weizsaecker, Hund, Heckmann, Gardner, Prigogine and Stengers.) [German]

Ambrose E.J., "The Mirror of Creation", Scottish Academic Press, Edinburgh, 1990.

Atkins P.W., "The Creation", W.H.Freeman and Comp., Oxford and San Francisco, 1981.

Barbour Ian, "Issues in Science and Religion", Harper Torchbooks, Harper and Row, New York, 1966.

Barbour Ian, "Myths, Models and Paradigms", Harper and Row, New York, 1974.

Barbour Ian, "Religion in an Age of Science", Harper and Row, San Francisco, 1990.

Barrett Eric and Fischer David, "Scientists Who Believe" (21 tell their own stories.)The Moody Bible Institute of Chicago, 1984.

Barclay Oliver, ed., "Christian Faith and Science", UCCF Associates for Christians in Science, Leicester, 1988.

Barrow John and Silk Joseph, "The Left Hand of Creation", Basic Books, New York, 1983.

Barrow John and Tipler Frank, "The Anthropic Cosmological Principle", Oxford Univ. Press, New York, 1986.

Baroow John, "The World Within the World", Oxford Univ.Press, Oxford, 1990.

Barrow John, "Theories of Everything", Oxford University Press, Oxford, 1991.

Bartholomew David, "God of Chance", SCM Press, London, 1984.

Bavink Bernhard, "Weltschoepfung", Ernst Reinhard Verlag, Munchen/Basel, 1951. [German]

Bergson Henri, "The Creative Mind", The Wisdom Library, Division of Philosophical Library, New York, 1946.

Bergson Henri, "Time and Free Will", Harper and Row, 1960.

Bergson Henri, "Creative Evolution", University Press of America, Lanham, 1983.

Berry R.J., ed., "Real Science, Real Faith", Monarch, Eastbourne, 1991.

Boeckle Franz, Kaufman Franz-Xaver, Rahner Karl, Welte Bernhard, eds., "Christliche Glaube im moderner Gesellschaft", Herder, Freiburg, Basel, Wien, 1980.1982, 1988. [German]
Teilband 3.(Rawer Karl, Rahner Karl:"Weltall-Erde-Mensch";Bosshard Stefan Niklaus:"Evolution und Schoepfung";Hassenstein Bernard:"Tier und Mensch";

SCIENCE AND FAITH

Meyer-Abich Klaus M.:"Natur und Geschichte".)
Teilband 4.(Meyer-Abich Klaus M.:"Determination und Freiheit";Rawer Karl, Pesch Otto Hemann:"Kausalitat-Zufall-Vorsehung";Weissmahr Bela, Knoch Otto:"Naturliche Phänomene und Wunder".)
Teilband 20. (Schaeffler Richard:"Wissenschaftstheorie und Theologie";Altner Günter, "Technisch- wissenschaftliche Welt und Schoepfung";Boeckle Franz, von Eiff August Wilhelm:"Wissenschaft und Ethos".)

Bohm David, "Wholeness and the Implicate Order", Ark Paperbacks, London and New York, 1980, 1983.

Bosshard Niklaus Stefan, "Erschafft die Welt sich selbst?" Herder, Freiburg, 1987. [German]

Boeker Werner, "Der Sinn von Evolution", Patmos Verlag, Dusseldorf, 1967. [German]

Burger Dionys, "Sphereland" (A Fantasy About Curved Spaces and an Expanding Universe), Thomas Crowell Co., New York, 1965.

Cantore Enrico, "Scientific Man", ISH Publications, New York, 1977.(Institute for Scientific Humanism, Lowenstein Center at Fordham University, New York)

Carré A.M., ed., "Pour Vous, qui est Jesus-Christ?", Les Edition du Cerf, 1971. [French]

Carvin W.P., "Creation and Scientific Explanation", Scottish Academic Press, Edinburgh, 1988.

Clark Gordon, "The Philosophy of Science and Belief in God",
Craig Press, Nutley, New Jersey, 1977.

Chaisson Eric, "The Life Era", The Atlantic Monthly Press, New York, 1987.

Conrad-Martius und Emmrich Curt, "Das Lebendige, Die Endlichkeit der Welt, Der Mensch", Hochland Bucherei, Koessel Verlag, München, 1951. [German]

Custance Arthur, "Two Men Called Adam", Arthur Custance, Brockville, Ontario, Canada.

Davies Paul, "Other Worlds", A Touchstone Book, Simon and Schuster, 1980, 1982.

Davies Paul, "The Accidental Universe, ", Cambridge University Press, Cambridge, 1982, 1986.

Davies Paul, "God and the New Physics", J.M.Dent and Sons, London and Melbourne, 1983.

Davies Paul, "Superforce", Touchstone Book, Simon and Schuster, New York, 1984.

Davies Paul, "The Cosmic Blueprint", Simon and Schuster, 1988.

Davies Paul, "The Mind of God", Simon and Schuster, New York, 1992.

Dessauer Friedrich, "Religion im Lichte der heutigen Naturwissenschaft", Verlag Josef Knecht, Frankfurt am Main, 1956. [German]

Dessauer Friedrich, "Auf den Spuren der Unendlichkeit", Verlag Josef Knecht, Frankfurt am Main, 1958. [German]

Dürr Hans-Peter, ed., "Physik und Transzendenz". Die grossen Physiker unseres Jahrhunderts uber ihre Begegnung mit dem Wunderbaren.(Planck, Jeans, Einstein, Born, Eddington, Bohr, Schroedinger, Pauli, Jordan, von Weizsacker, Bohm, Heisenberg).Scherz Verlag, Bern, München, Wien, 1988. [German]

Dyson Freeman, "Disturbing the Universe", Basic Books, New York, 1979.

Dyson Freeman, "Infinite in all Directions", Harper and Row, 1985.

Dyson Freeman, "Origins of Life", Cambridge University Press, Cambridge, 1985, 1988.

Einstein Albert, "Ideas and Opinions", Bonanza Books, New York, 1954.

Select Bibliography

Einstein Albert, "Out of My Later Years", The Citadel Press, Secaucus, New Jersey, 1950, 1979.

Hoffmann Banesh, "Albert Einstein Creator and Rebel, " A Plume Book, New American Library, New York, 1972.

Dukas Helen and Hoffmann Banesh, "Albert Einstein, The Human Side", Princeton University Press, Princeton, 1979.

Calder Nigel, "Einstein's Universe", Penguin Books, 1980, 1986.

Evans Stephen, "The Quest for Faith", Inter-Varsity Press, Downers Grove, Illinois, 1986.

Fagg Lawrence, "Two Faces of Time", The Theosophical Publishing House, Wheaton(Illinois), Madras, London, 1985.

Fischer Robert, "God did it, but how?", Academic Books, Grand Rapids, Michigan, 1981.

Frankenberger Ernst, "Gottbekenntnisse grosser Naturforscher", Johannes-Verlag, Leutesdorf am Rhein, 1969, 1973. [German]

Gamow George, "One Two Three...Infinity", Bantam Books, New York, 1957, 1961.

Gassen Karl, "Geplante Ewigkeit" (Naturwissenschaft-Religion-Evolution), Verlag Pfeiffer, München, 1987. [German]

Gleick James, "Chaos", Penguin Books, 1987.

Goez Wilhelm, "Naturwissenschaft und Evangelium", Quelle und Meyer, Heidelbnerg, 1954. [German]

Gribbin John, "Genesis", Delta, Eleanor Friede Book, New York, 1981.

Gribbin John and Rees Martin, "Cosmic Coincidences", Bantam Books, New York, 1989.

Haas Johannes, "Biologie und Gottesglaube", Morus Verlag, Berlin, 1961. [German]

Hayward Alan, "God is" (A scientist shows why it makes sense to believe in God), Thomas Nelson Publishers, Nashville, New York, 1978, 1980.

Hayward Alan, "God's Truth" (A scientist shows why it makes sense to believe the Bible), Thomas Nelson Publishers, Nashville, New York, 1973, 1983.

Heisenberg Werner, "Physik und Philosophie", S.Hirzel Verlag, Stuttgart 1959. [German]

Heisenber Werner, "Physics and Beyond", Harper Torchbooks, Harper and Row, 1971.

Heisenberg Werner, "Across the Frontiers", Harper and Row, New York, 1974.

Heitler Walter, "Der Mensch und die naturwissenschaftliche Erklenntnis", Vieweg, Braunschweig, 1961, 1970. [German]

Heitler Walter, "Naturphilosophiphische Streifzuge." Vieweg, Braunschwig, 1970. [German]

Heitler Walter, "Die Natur und das Göttliche"Verlag Klett und Balmer, Zug, 1974. [German]

Henry Carl, ed., "Horizons of Science"(Christian Scholars Speak out), Harper and Row, 1978.

Houghton John, "Does God Play Dice?", Inter-Varsity Press, Leicester, UK, 1989.

Houston J., "Is it reasonable to believe in God?", The Handsel Press, Edinburgh, 1984.

Hooykaas R., "Religion and the Rise of Modern Science", William Eerdmans Publ., Grand Rapids, Michigan, 1972.

SCIENCE AND FAITH

Hübner Jürgen, "Der Dialog zwischen Theologie und Naturwissenschaft" (Ein bibliographischer Bericht), Chr.Kaiser Verlag, Munchen, 1987. [German]

Hunger Edgar, "Von Demokrit bis Heisenberg", Friedr.Vieweg and Sohn, Braunschweig, 1964. [German]

Hyers Conrad, "The Meaning of Creation"(Genesis and Modern Science), John Knox Press, Atlanta, 1984.

Illies Joachim, "Die Welt ist Gottes Schoepfung", Herderbücherei, Freiburg im Breisgau, 1981, 1983. [German]

Jaki Stanley, "Cosmos and Creator", Gateway Edition, Regnery Gateway, Chicago, 1980.

Jaki Stanley, "Science and Creation", Scottish Academic Press, Edinburgh, 1986.

Jastrow Robert, "God and the Astronomers", Warner Books Edition, New York, 1978.

Jeans James, "Physics and Philosophy", Cambridge University Press, 1946.

Jordan Pascual, "Atom und Weltall", Vieweg, Braunschweig, 1956. [German]

Jordan Pascual, "Der Naturwissenschaftler vor der religioesen Frage", Gerhard Stalling Verlag, Oldenburg/Hamburg, 1963.1972. [German]

Kurtua R., ed., "Chto govoryat o Boge sovremennie ucheniye", Impremerie A.Rosseels, Louvain, Belgique, 1960 ("Life with God", Brussels, Belgium, 1960) [Russian]

Lang-Sims Lois, "One thing only" (A Christian Guide to the Universal Quest for God), Paragon House, New York, 1988.

Luyten Norbert, ed. "Fuhrt ein Weg zu Gott?"(Dominique Dubarle, Heimo Dolch, Herbert Doms, Norbert Luyten, Joseph Meurers, Beda Thum), Verlag Karl Alber, Freiburg/Munchen, 1972. [German]

Luyten Norbert, ed., "Zufall, Freiheit, Vorsehung"(August von Eiff, Norbert Luyten, August Meessen, Leo Scheffczyk, Beda Thum, Wolfgang Wickler), Verlag Karl Alber, Freiburg/Munchen, 1975 [German]

Mackay Donald, "The Clockwork Image", Inter-Varsity Press, Downers Grove, Illinois, 1974.

Mallove Eugene, "The Quickening Universe", St.Martin's Press, New York, 1987.

Magnum John, ed., "The New Faith-Science Debate", (Probing Cosmology, Technology and Theology), Fortress Press, Minneapolis, 1989.

Margenau Henry, "The Miracle of Existence", New Science Library, Boston and London, 1987.

Maritain Jacques, "Wege zur Gotteserkenntnis", (Titel des Originals:"Approches de Dieu")Verlag Alsatia, Paris, [German]

Maurin Krzysztof, Michalski Krzysztof, Enno Rudolph, eds. "Offene Systeme II" (Logik und Zeit), Klett-Cotta, Stuttgart, 1981 [German]

McIntyre John, "The Appeal of Christianity to a Scientist", Inter-Varsity Press, Madison, WI, 1974.

McKinney Richard, ed., "Creation, Christ and Culture" (Studies in Honour of T.F.Torrance), T.and T.Clark Ltd., Edinburgh, 1976.

Mehlberg Henry, "Time, Causality and the Quantum Theory", D.Reidel Publ., Dodrecht, Holland (Boston, London) 1980.

Michalski Krzysztof, ed., "Der Mensch in den modernen Wissenschaften" (Castelgandolfo-Gespräche 1983), Klett- Cotta Verlag, Stuttgart, 1985. [German]

Michalski Krzysztof, ed., "Uber die Krise" (Castelgandolfo-Gesprache 1985), Klett-Cotta Verlag, Stuttgart, 1986.[German]

Select Bibliography

Mitchell Ralph, "Einstein and Christ", Scottish Academic Press, Edinburgh, 1987.

Morris Henry, "Men of Science - Men of God", Master Books, El Cajon, CA, 1988.

Morris Richard, "Time's Arrows", A Touchstone Book, Simon and Schuster, New York, 1985.

Mortensen Viggo and Sorensen Robert, "Free Will and Determinism", Aarhus University Press, Aarhus, Denmark, 1987.

Sir Mott Nevill, ed., "Can Scientists Believe?" James and James, London, 1991.

Muschalek Hubert, "Urmensch-Adam", Morus Verlag, Berlin, 1963. [German]

Muschalek Hubert, "Gottbekenntnisse Moderner Naturforscher", Morus Verlag, Berlin, 1964. [German]

Nebelsick Harold, "Theology and Science in Mutual Modification", Oxford University Press, New York, 1981.

Nebelsick Harold, "Circles of God", Scottish Academic Press, Edinburgh, 1985.

Lecompte du Noüy, "Human Destiny", Longmans, Green and Co., New York, 1947;also Signet Books, New York, 1949.

Osborn Denis, "The Andromedans"(and other Parables of Science and Faith), Inter-Varsity Press, Downers Grove, Illinois, 1977.

Pagels Heinz, "The Cosmic Code"(Physics as the Language of Nature), Michael Joseph, London, 1983.

Pagels Heinz, "Perfect Symmetry" (The search for the beginning of time), Bantam Books, Toronto, New York, 1985, 1986.

Paul Iain, "Science and Theology in Einstein's Perspective" Scottish Academic Press, Edinburgh, 1986.

Paul Iain, "Knowledge of God [Calvin, Einstein and Polanyi]" Scottish Academic Press, Edinburgh, 1987.

Peacocke Arthur, "Intimations of Reality" (Critical Realism in Science and Religion), University of Notre Dame Press, Notre Dame, 1984.

Peat David, "The Philosopher's Stone", Bantam Books, New York, 1991.

Peck Scott, "The Road Less Traveled" (A new psychology of love, traditional values and spiritual growth), A Touchstone Book, Simon and Schuster, New York, 1978.

Pieper Josef, "Über das Ende der Zeit" (Eine geschichts-philosophische Betrachtung), Koessel Verlag, Munchen, 1950, 1980. [German]

Polkinghorne John, "The Way the World is" (The Christian Perspective of a Scientist), William Eerdmans Publ., Grand Rapids, Michigan, 1983.

Polkinghorne John, "One World : The Interaction of Science and Theology", Princeton Univ.Press, Princeton, 1986.

Polkinghorne John, "Science and Creation" (The Search for Understanding), New Science Library, Boston, 1989.

Polkinghorne John, "Science and Providence"(God's Interaction with the World), New Science Library, 1989.

Pollard W.G., "Transcendence and Providence" (Reflections of a Physicist and Priest), Scottish Academic Press, 1987.

Prigogine Ilya, "From Being to Becoming", Freeman and Co., New York, San Francisco, 1980.

Prigogine Ilya and Stengers Isabelle, "Order out of Chaos", New Science Library, Boulder and London, 1984.

SCIENCE AND FAITH

Rauh Fritz, "Theologische Grenzfrage zur Biologie und Anthropologie", Don Bosco Verlag, Munchen, 1973. [German]

Redmond D.D., "The Existence of God", Catholic Truth Society, London, 1971.

Rohrbach Hans, "Naturwissenschaft, Weltbild, Glaube", Brockhaus Verlag, Wuppertal, 1975. [German]

Rohrbach Hans, "Das anstoessige Glaubensbekenntnis"(Ein Naturwissenschaftler zum christlichen Glaubensbekenntnis), Brunnen Verlag, Giessen, 1987. [German]

Russell Robert, Stoeger William, Coyne George, eds., "Physics, Philosophy and Theology : A common Quest for Understanding", Vatican Observatory - Vatican City State, University of Notre Dame Press, Notre Dame, 1988.

Schaeffer Francis, "The God Who is There"Inter-Varsity Press, Downers Grove, Illinois, 1979.

Schindler David, ed., "Beyond Mechanism"(The Universe in Recent Physics and Catholic Thought), University Press of America, Lanham, New York, London, 1986.

Schoffeniels E., "Anti-Chance" (A Reply to Monod's Chance and Necessity), Pergamon Press, Oxford, 1976 [Trans. "L'Anti- Hasard", Gauthier-Villars, Bordas, 1973.]

Schroeder Gerald, "Genesis and the Big Bang"(The Discovery of Harmony between Modern Science and the Bible), Bantam Books, New York 1990, 1992.

Schroedinger Erwin, "What is Life" and "Mind and Matter", Cambridge University Press, Cambridge, 1944, 1977.

Schumacher Heinz, "Urknall und Schoepfergott", R.Brockhaus Verlag, Wupertal und Zürich, 1990. [German]

Sheldrake Rupert, "A New Science of Life" (The Hypothesis of Formative Causation), J.P.Tarcher, Los Angeles, 1987 [Originally publ. : Blond and Briggs, London, 1981.]

Silk Joseph, "The Big Bang", W.H.Freeman and Co., San Francisco, 1980.

Spaemann Heinrich, ed., "Wer ist Jesus von Nazaret - fur mich?" (100 zeitgenoessische Zeugnisse), Koessel Verlag, Munchen, 1978. [German]

Stannard Russel, "Grounds for Reasonable Belief", Scottish Academic Press, Edinburgh, 1989.

Stuhlhofer Franz, "Naturforscher und die Frage nach Gott", Schwengeler Verlag, Berneck, 1988. [German]

Teilhard de Chardin Pierre, "The Phenomenon of Man", Harper Colophone Books, Harper and Row, New York.1959, 1975.

Teilhard de Chardin Pierre, "Hymn of The Universe", Collins, Fount, London, 1961, 1981.

R.Wayne Kraft, "A Reason to Hope : A Synthesis of Teilhard de Chardin's Vision and System Thinking", Intersystems Publications, Seaside, California 1983.

Templeton John, "The Humble Approach"(Scientists Discover God), The Seabury Press, New York, 1981.

Templeton John, Herrmann Robert, "The God Who Would Be Known", Harper and Row, New York, 1989.

Thaxton Charles, Bradley Walter, Olsen Roger, "The Mystery of Life's Origin", Philosophical Library, New York, 1984.

Torrance Thomas, "Reality and Scientific Theology", Scottish Academic Press, Edinburgh, 1985.

Select Bibliography

Torrance Thomas, "The Christian Frame of Mind" (Reason, order and openness in theology and natural science), Helmers and Howard, Colorado Springs, 1989.

Toulmin Stephen, "The return to Cosmology", University of California Press, Berkeley, Los Angeles, London, 1982.

Trinklein Frederick, "The God of Science", William Eerdmans Publ., Grand Rapids, Michigan, 1971.

Trutwin Werner, ed., Theologisches Forum, "Religion und Wissenschaft", Patmos Verlag, Dusseldorf, 1970 [German]

Van Till Howard, "The Fourth Day" (What the Bible and the Heavens Are Telling us about the Creation), William Eerdmans Publ., Grand Rapids, Michigan, 1987.

Varghese Abraham, ed., "The Intellectuals speak out about God", Regnery Gateway, Chicago, 1984.

von Weizsaecker Carl Friedrich, "Die Tragweite der Wissenschaft"(Schoepfung und Weltenstehung), S.Hirzel Verlag, Stuttgart, 1966. [German]

von Weizsaecker Carl Friedrich, "Zum Weltbild der Physik", S.Hirzel Verlag, Stuttgart, 1970.

von Weizsaecker Carl Friedrich, "Die Einheit der Natur", Carl Hanser Verlag, Munchen, 1971.

Whitehead Alfred North, "Science and the Modern World", The Free Press, A Division of the Macmillan Comp., New York, 1925, 1967.

Whittaker Edmund, "Der Anfang und das Ende der Welt"(Die Dogmen und die Naturgesetze), Gunther Verlag, Stuttgart, 1955. [German]

Wicken Jeffrey, "Evolution, Thermodynamics and Information", Oxford University Press, Oxford, 1987.

Wilber Ken, ed., "Quantum Questions"(Wilber, Heisenberg, Schroedinger, Einstein, De Broglie, Jeans, Planck, Pauli, Eddington), New Science Library, Boston and London, 1985.

Young Arthur, "Der Kreative Kosmos", Koessel Verlag, Munchen, 1976, 1987. [German]

Zoller Heinrich, ed., "Die Befreiung von wissenschaftlichen Glauben", Herderbucherei, Freiburg im Breisgau, 1974. [German]

SCIENCE AND FAITH

INDEX OF AUTHORS

Alyea, Hubert	32
Ampère, André Maria	14
Arseniev, Nikolai	93
St. Augustine	39, 84, 93
Barbour, Ian	32, 79
Barrow, John	52
Bergson, Henri	49
Berry, Sam	81
Berzelius, Jons Jacob	15
Bohr, Niels	23, 24, 25, 26, 28
Bonhoeffer, Dietrich	6
Boskovic, Rudjer	14
Boyd, Robert	77, 91
Bube, Richard	6
Cantore, Enrico	31
Carr, B.J.	52
Carrel, Alexis	21
Carter, Brandon	52
Cauchy, Augustin Louis	15
Chaisson, Eric	91
Compton, Arthur	21
Corwin, Mike	56
Darwin, Charles	65, 74, 78
Davies, Paul	49, 81
Demianski, Mark	57
Dessauer, Friedrich	10
Dionysion-Kouimtzi, Semiramis	77
Dyson, Freeman	56
Eddington, Arthur	28, 85
Einstein, Albert	10, 27, 28, 33, 40, 63
Euler, Leonhard	95
Faraday, Michael	15, 16
Gamow, George	39

SCIENCE AND FAITH

Gribbin, John	33
Gauss, Karl Friedrich	14
Hayward, Alan	76
Heisenberg, Werner	12, 22, 23, 26, 28
Heitler, Walter	9, 12, 22, 24, 49, 72
Heraclitus	72
Herschel, William	14
Hoyle, Fred	55
Jastrow, Robert	92
Jeans, James	21
Jordan, Pascual	22, 24, 26
Joule, Prescot James	17
Kelvin (Lord Thomson), William	17, 18
Kepler, Johannes	11, 12
Kopernik, Nikolaj	11, 12
Kraft, R.Wayne	78
von Laue, Max	20
Leibniz, Gottfried Wielhelm	13
von Liebig, Justus	16
von Linné, Karl	14
Livingstone, David	19
Lomonosov, Mikhail	5
Lousma, Jack	32
Lovell, Bernard	53
Lyell, Charles	16
Maedler, Heinrich	16
Marconi, Guglielmo	30
Maxwell, James Clerk	16, 62
Mayer, Robert	17
Miller, Andrew	72, 73
Millikan, Robert	20
Nernst, Walter	17, 18
Newton, Isaac	12, 13, 29
du Noüy, Pierre Lecomte	31
Oersted, Hans	14
Pascal, Blaise	5
Pavlov, Ivan	92
Pauli, Wolfgang	23, 35, 66
Peacocke, Arthur	70, 79, 90
Planck, Max	18, 19, 22, 25, 90
Poincaré, Henri	61, 62
Polkinghorne, John	5, 79, 82
Prigogine, Ilya	61, 62, 63, 64, 65, 66, 68, 69, 70, 74, 86
Pupin, Mihailo	30

Index of Authors

Lord Rayleigh (John William Strutt)	16
Rees, Martin	33, 52
Reinke, Johannes	19
Rolston III, Holmes	49
Rutherford, Ernest	20, 26
Sabatier, Paul	21
Schroedinger, Erwin	22, 25, 26
Shelley, Perry Bysshe	7
Spinoza, Baruch	11
Stengers, Isabelle	61, 65, 66
Teilhard de Chardin, Pierre	49, 77, 78
Tipler, Frank	52
Torrance, Thomas	79, 80
Vogt, Heinrich	22
Wald, George	57
Ware, Kalistos	95
Weisskopf, Victor	76

Quotations from the Bible

Psalms, 19/1-4	4
Matthew, 6/10	83
Luke, 13/18, 19	83
Romans, 1/20	4
1 Corinthians, 13/4-6	94
13/8	93
2 Peter, 3/8	76
1 John, 4/8, 16	4
4/16	93

SCIENCE AND FAITH